D0375039

Air Pollution

PROBLEMS AND SOLUTIONS

J. S. Kidd and Renee A. Kidd

CHELSEA HOUSE
PUBLISHERS
An imprint of Infobase Publishing

This one is for Loren.

✦

Chelsea House
An imprint of Infobase Publishing
132 West 31st Street
New York NY 10001

ISBN-13: 978-0-8160-5605-7
ISBN-10: 0-8160-5605-6

Library of Congress Cataloging-in-Publication Data
Kidd, J. S. (Jerry S.)
   Air pollution : problems and solutions / J. S. Kidd and Renee A. Kidd.
      p. cm.
   Rev. ed. of: Into thin air. 1998.
   Includes bibliographical references and index.
   ISBN 0-8160-5605-6
   1. Air—Pollution. I. Kidd, Renee A. II. Kidd, J. S. (Jerry S.) Into thin air.
III. Title.

   TD883.K47 2005
   363.739′2—dc22   2005052791

Chelsea House books are available at special discounts when purchased in bulk quantities for businesses, associations, institutions, or sales promotions. Please call our Special Sales Department in New York at (212) 967-8800 or (800) 322-8755.

You can find Chelsea House on the World Wide Web at http://www.chelseahouse.com

Text design by James Scotto-Lavino
Cover design by Pehrsson Design
Illustrations by Sholto Ainsle

Printed in the United States of America

MP Hermitage 10 9 8 7 6 5 4 3 2

This book is printed on acid-free paper.

Contents

Preface

The products of science and technology influence the lives of all citizens, including young adults. New means of communication and transportation, new ways of doing work and pursuing recreation, new foods, and new medicines arrive almost daily. Science also engenders new ways of looking at the world and at other citizens. Likewise, science can raise concerns about moral and ethical values.

Dealing with all such changes requires some resiliency. The needed adaptations by individuals are fostered by knowledge of the inner workings of science and technology and of the researchers and engineers who do the studies and design the products. Consequently, one of the goals of the Science and Society set of books is to illuminate these subjects in a way that is both accurate and understandable.

One of the obstacles in reaching that goal is the fact that almost all the connections between citizens and scientists are impersonal. For example, the direction of study in a specialized field of science is now mainly determined by negotiations between the leaders of research projects and government officials. National elections rarely hinge on questions of science and technology. Such matters are usually relegated to secondary political status. In any case, most of the officials who are concerned with science are not elected but are appointed and are members of large government bureaucracies.

Other influences on the directions taken by science and technology come from other bureaucratic organizations such as international political bodies, large commercial firms, academic institutions, or philanthropic foundations. However, in recent years, influence has also come from more informal voluntary groups of citizens and citizen action organizations. The scope of the set has been revised to reflect the growing importance of such channels linking citizens to the leaders in science.

The books describe some of the dramatic adventures on the part of the people who do scientific work, show some of the human side of science, and convey the idea that scientists experience the kinds of day-to-day frustrations that everyone does.

The revisions attempt to show some of the developing trends in the impact of science on sections of the citizenry such as groupings by age or gender—or geographic location. An example is the change in the living conditions in small, rural communities that have come about as a consequence of agricultural mechanization. Finally, the books describe some of the significant strides in the actual findings of science in recent years. Some fields of science such as genetics and molecular biology have gone through a virtual revolution. These radical changes are ongoing. Likewise, the development of natural medicines was recently given social prominence by the establishment of government agencies devoted explicitly to the support of such research.

Science and Society shows the extent to which individuals can have a stake in the enterprise called science and technology—how they can cope with the societal changes entailed and how they can exert some personal influence on what is happening.

Acknowledgments

W e thank the faculty and staff of the College of Information Studies at the University of Maryland, College Park—particularly Diane Barlow. Professor Alistair B. Fraser at the Pennsylvania State University gave us some cogent advice as did Dick Feely at the Pacific Marine Environmental Laboratory, National Oceanic and Atmospheric Administration, Seattle, Washington. Gwen Pitman of CCI, Inc., and Amy Ballard of the Smithsonian Institution helped us find useful images. We also want to offer special thanks to the librarians at the University of Maryland and at the National Research Council in Washington, D.C., for their consistent support.

Introduction

Air Pollution is a revised edition of our previous book on the same subject called *Into Thin Air*. Since that title was used for a book about mountain climbing, a new, less confusing title for the present book was adopted. *Air Pollution* is a simple title with an ambitious goal—to articulate the need for political leaders to make important social and economic decisions that result in a balance between the goal of a healthy environment and the goal of economic prosperity.

A specific objective of the present book is to show how scientists and engineers are working to help policy makers solve the problems of atmospheric pollution. Scientific research illuminates the causes of air pollution—both natural and from human activities. It shows how pollution is distributed from sources to final destinations. Scientific research also reveals the consequences of pollution—for human health, for the economy, and for the health of animals and plants in our environment.

Several scientific disciplines contribute to our knowledge about air pollution. For example, atmospheric chemists were the first to note the fact that some gases used in commercial products were reacting with the stratospheric ozone that protects people from the most harmful of the Sun's radiations. Mathematicians and physicists first recognized that some kinds of air turbulence could be described by mathematical equations. Meteorologists extended that idea and devised the first mathematical models of the weather—tools that ultimately allowed them to produce highly accurate weather forecasts. Similarly, climatologists expanded the idea of modeling to encompass the whole world and vast spans of time. Meanwhile, engineers were developing equipment such as catalytic converters that could reduce the emission of nitrogen oxides from automobile exhaust systems. Engineering technology is seen as the means to reduce or eliminate pollution at the source and the ways to recover from polluted conditions from any cause.

After the first version of this book was published, significant changes in the air pollution situation have occurred. From a practical perspective, the most important appear to be the reductions in the levels of sulfur oxides, nitrogen oxides and lead in the air. Sulfur oxides are notorious for their role in the making of acid rain. These gases come mainly from burning coal to produce electricity. By the late 1990s, government officials were able to establish a program of agreements with the managers of electric power plants. The program specified an upper limit (called a "cap") on sulfur oxide emissions. The cap was to gradually get smaller over several years.

The limits were based on the particular history of pollution for each individual power plant. If a specific plant exceeded its limit, the managers were required to pay a monetary penalty. If a plant produced less pollution than its allowance called for, the managers could sell their surplus pollution permits to the managers of other power plants. Remarkably, this program has resulted in a decline of between 20 and 30 percent in total national sulfur dioxide emissions.

Nitrogen oxides also come from burning coal and other fuels, but the most significant source is automobile and truck exhaust. There is no allowance program for nitrogen oxides, but nitrogen oxide pollution has also declined. Since coal is in the picture, some of the decline is probably tied to the changes induced by the new controls on sulfur. However, most of the decline in nitrogen oxides is linked to the adoption of exhaust gas processing—including reburning of exhaust as well as the use of the catalytic converters.

Lead reductions appear to have come about in a similar way. The electric power plants' pollution reduction equipment works to some extent on all three pollutants, but the use of unleaded gasoline is probably the main factor.

Other good news has been provided by the decline in the production and use of chlorofluorocarbons (CFCs). Manufacturers in the United States stopped production of CFCs even before the Environmental Protection Agency (EPA) established a formal ban on production and use. However, problems remain because of continuing production and use in less industrialized countries. Also, CFC smuggling has become a law enforcement problem and, unfortunately, the new CFC substitutes appear to be powerful greenhouse gases.

Still other favorable developments have included the adoption of strict controls on particles in the atmosphere. Research on the role of asbestos and other mineral particles in lung disease revealed that all kinds of microscopic particles are health hazards. Officials of the EPA have recently announced restrictions on particle emissions from diesel engines in cars and trucks and in stationary installations.

Probably the most stubborn air pollution problem is carbon dioxide. The production of carbon dioxide continues to rise, and only minor remedies are available. The possible bright spot in the carbon dioxide picture comes from improvements in the accuracy and scope of both weather and climate information. Many of these improvements have come from the better design and use of orbital satellites. If the global climate is changing because of the rise in carbon dioxide levels, more accurate and timelier warnings of such changes will be forthcoming from the new weather- and climate-measuring instruments.

Air Pollution continues the effort to show how science and technology are being used to help solve society's problems. Emphasis is also given to the role of citizens in pushing for an atmospheric environment that is as clean as possible.

1
The Atmosphere

Atmospheres are composed of gases. These gases are some-times made up of single atoms such as neon but more often are composed of compound molecules such as natural oxygen, which consists of two oxygen atoms. In addition to oxygen, the air we breathe contains nitrogen molecules, made of two atoms of nitrogen. (Its symbol is N_2.) (The small number after the elements' symbols indicates how many atoms of that element are necessary to form the molecule.) Some of the gases in the Earth's atmosphere are made up of two different elements. Carbon dioxide (CO_2), for example, is composed of one atom of carbon joined with two atoms of oxygen.

Atmospheres in the Solar System

The Moon, our nearest astronomical neighbor, cannot hold an atmosphere because its small size does not provide sufficient gravity to hold even heavy gases. The gravitational pull of our small Moon is no match for the mighty tug of the vacuum of interplanetary space. Any gases that might have been present when the Moon was formed were sucked into deep space millions of years ago.

Mars, called the Red Planet, has a very thin atmosphere. The planet is barely large enough and dense enough to hold a wispy mixture of gases. However, Venus, known as the Morning Star,

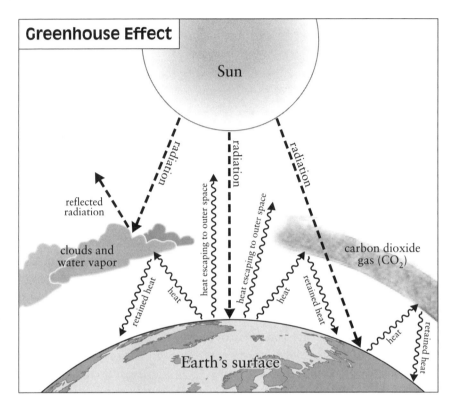

Greenhouse Effect

Sun

reflected radiation

clouds and water vapor

carbon dioxide gas (CO_2)

Earth's surface

radiation

heat escaping to outer space

retained heat

heat

The greenhouse effect is caused when CO_2, water vapor and other gases block the escape of radiant energy from near the Earth's surface.

is large and dense enough to hold a thick layer of gas on its surface. This gas is a toxic mixture of carbon dioxide with a dash of nitrogen and some sulfur compounds. At surface level, the gas is hot enough to melt lead. This superheated temperature exists because Venus is nearer to the Sun than Earth is. In addition, the thick layer of carbon dioxide gas traps much of the sun's radiant energy and keeps the intense heat close to the surface of Venus.

This process is known as the "greenhouse effect." Most of the Sun's rays pass through the carbon dioxide layer and reach the surface of the planet. The surface absorbs some of the energy and generates heat. The heat is reradiated skyward, but the carbon dioxide blocks the upward movement. The CO_2 holds the heat and sends it back toward the surface. Therefore, the heat energy is trapped between the CO_2 layer in the atmosphere and the surface of the planet.

In contrast to its neighbors, Earth's atmosphere is about 80 percent nitrogen. The nitrogen molecule, N_2, is a very placid molecule that does not react easily with other chemicals. Oxygen and small traces of other gases make up the other 20 percent of the atmosphere. These trace gases include a small amount of carbon dioxide. The carbon dioxide holds enough heat energy near the surface of the Earth to allow the planet to support life. This trace amount of CO_2, about .003 percent, is far less than that in the Venusian atmosphere.

Earth's Atmospheric Changes

Earth's atmosphere has evolved over time and continues to do so. The original atmosphere of the hot, newborn Earth was probably a mixture of hydrogen and helium. The hydrogen and helium atoms are the smallest of all the elements. Molecules composed of these elements are lighter than air—think of how a helium-filled balloon will quickly rise skyward. As the Earth cooled, hydrogen and helium were sucked away by the vacuum of outer space.

During the next stage of atmospheric evolution, heavier gases—ammonia, containing nitrogen and hydrogen, and methane, containing carbon and hydrogen—were the main components. These heavier gases arose from deep within the Earth and escaped from volcanoes, vents, and geysers. Scientists believe that such gases provided the raw materials for the first life on Earth. A current theory suggests that life originated in water containing molecules of ammonia and methane. The development of life was activated by sunlight and, perhaps, lightning. According to this theory, the first life-forms were probably simple molecules assembled from the ammonia and methane. These molecules were able to reproduce themselves. Eventually, such molecules formed a protective skin or membrane and became one-celled creatures.

There was little, if any, oxygen in that second period of the earth's atmosphere. In fact, atmospheric oxygen probably would have been poisonous to these primitive creatures. Over eons of time, the atmosphere changed and the proportions of oxygen and molecular nitrogen increased as the reaction of ammonia and water released both gases. The ammonia (NH_2) yielded the nitrogen that dominates the present atmosphere. The water (H_2O) gave up part of its oxygen in the process. The methane (CH_4) was transformed into carbon dioxide (by bonding with oxygen). Other carbon-based molecules were washed out of the air by rain. Slowly, the atmosphere became richer in oxygen.

In the meantime, some of the primitive life-forms that existed in the ammonia-and-methane period migrated to an oxygen-free environment in the deep sea or far underground. Their successors still exist in such places. Other single-celled creatures adapted to the gradually increasing proportion of oxygen in the air. Those that adapted to oxygen became the forerunners of all the multicelled plants and animals that now occupy the Earth.

The Seasons

Scientists are not always serious. One atmospheric chemist remarked that the Earth enjoys the "Goldilocks" condition. Our planet is not too hot, not too cold, but just right. Of course, that scientist was referring to ideal conditions for life. An essential life-supporting condition is the availability of liquid water. Water (H_2O) comes in three forms. Solid water is ice, gaseous water is steam or water vapor, and liquid water is the substance that is needed for life. Ice becomes liquid when it is heated, and liquid water becomes a gas when it evaporates. The evaporation of a liquid is hastened by heat, and steam forms when the temperature of the liquid is raised to its boiling point (240 degrees Fahrenheit, 100 degrees Celsius). On some planets, the cold is so intense that water (if there is any) is frozen solid. On other planets, the temperature is so hot that all water (if there is any) is in the form of water vapor or steam.

In our solar system, Earth appears to be the only planet that can sustain liquid water. There may be traces of water on Mars, but this water would be frozen solid. Mars has too little atmosphere to hold the Sun's heat and, therefore, is much too cold for liquid water. Some of the large moons that circle Jupiter and Saturn may have liquid water below a frozen surface. The telescope on the *Galileo* spacecraft has detected what appear to be ice floes on Europa, one of Jupiter's moons. If these ice floes indicate the presence of liquid water under a covering of ice, the warmth to keep it liquid is not supplied by the distant Sun. The heat probably results from long-term radioactivity. This action is similar to the process that forms lava by melting the rock below the Earth's solid crust.

In contrast to the other planets in the solar system, the average temperature of Earth is in the moderate range. This condition allows liquid water to exist over most of its surface. Although Earth's average temperature may be "just right," many places on Earth experience temperatures that vary greatly. Local weather conditions can change from hour to hour and as well as during seasonal weather cycles.

The seasons occur because the Earth is tilted on its axis. As the Earth circles the Sun, the direction of the tilt always remains the same. Winter comes to the Northern Hemisphere when the tilt of the axis moves the northern part of the Earth away from the Sun. Conversely, summer arrives when the northern half is tilted toward the Sun. The seasons in the

Southern Hemisphere are always the reverse of those in the Northern Hemisphere. When it is winter in New York, it is summer in Rio de Janeiro and vice versa.

In past times, those who studied geography divided the Earth into various regions. The surface of the Earth was divided into the Southern and Northern Hemispheres by an imaginary line called the equator. The equator is midway between the North Pole in the Arctic and the South Pole in the Antarctic. Three climate zones lie on each side of the equator. Tropical climate zones are found nearest the equator. Except near the tops of tall mountains, temperatures in the tropics rarely, if ever, fall below the freezing point of water. The temperate zones range between the tropics and the coldest areas. The temperate zones have the most pronounced seasonal changes in temperature, rainfall, and other variables. However, the average temperature is mild—about 60 degrees Fahrenheit or 15 degrees Celsius.

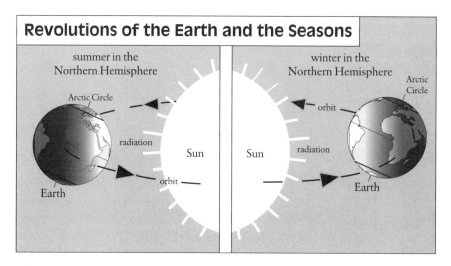

The Earth is tilted relative to the plane of its orbit around the Sun. Consequently, during winter in the Northern Hemisphere, the Arctic is dark in the daytime and the Antarctic region is lighted by the Sun even at night. When it is summer in the Northern Hemisphere, the opposite conditions exist.

The zones farthest from the equator and surrounding the North or South Poles are the Arctic zones. *Arctic* is a Greek word referring to the north. Because the scholars who wrote the original geography books lived in the Northern Hemisphere, they called the southern polar region the "Antarctic" or opposite to the Arctic. In the Arctic zones the temperature is consistently below the freezing point of water and most snow in the Arctic zones remains frozen. Each year, the previous snowfall is compacted into ice by the weight of the new snow. Thus, the Arctic zones are said to have a permanent ice cap.

In the tropical regions nearest the equator, there is no appreciable winter season. However, other changes take place in a rhythmic fashion. In the Caribbean area, the hurricane season starts in late June and lasts until November. Central America has a dry season from November to April and a wet season from May to October with a short dry spell in July.

Other areas of the globe experience yearly cycles of torrential rains known as monsoons. In India, for example, the monsoon seasons lasts from June through September. The rainy months are followed by a warm autumn, a mild winter, and a hot period from March through May.

Climate and Climate Change

All these rhythmic variations take place within a set of conditions called climate. The idea of climate represents a combination of factors such as temperature, humidity, and rainfall that follow general patterns in a given region. In what is described as a Mediterranean climate, the days are quite warm, the nights are chilly, and the temperature rarely falls to the freezing point of water. San Francisco, California, has a Mediterranean climate with the added peculiarity that the summer months may be slightly colder than the winter months because of shifting ocean currents.

In the study of climate, average temperature and average rainfall are the most important factors. Ireland provides a good example of a truly temperate climate. The range of temperatures is narrow. In the summer, the temperature rarely rises above 80 degrees Fahrenheit (27 degrees Celsius). When it does, the Irish are convinced that they are suffering from a heat wave. In the winter, some ice may form on still water at night, but water rarely freezes during the daytime. Indeed, year-round temperatures usually range between 50 and 70 degrees Fahrenheit (10–21 degrees Celsius). Although the temperature range is low, the amount of rainfall is high. The areas covered by natural vegetation remain green all year. Consequently, Ireland is called the Emerald Isle.

The average temperatures found in midwestern areas of the United States are somewhat misleading. Fairly extreme fluctuations frequently occur. For example, the temperature in central Indiana can reach more than 100 degrees Fahrenheit (38 degrees Celsius) in the summer and 10 degrees below zero Fahrenheit (minus 23 degrees Celsius) in the winter. Yet Indiana is considered to have a temperate climate with an average temperature of about 51 degrees Fahrenheit (11 degrees Celsius). Thus, although the average temperature is temperate—a mild, middle value—the extremes can be either tropical or arctic. In fact, the temperature in Indiana can change by 40 degrees Fahrenheit (22 degrees Celsius) overnight.

Scientists now fear that our changeable climate will change even more dramatically. The world faces the prospect that human activities are responsible for unpleasant weather modifications. Climatologists fear that the blanket of carbon dioxide gas found in the Venusian atmosphere may someday have a counterpart on Earth. As yet, Earth's blanket of carbon dioxide is much thinner than the one that keeps Venus unbearably hot. However, air pollution is slowly thickening the blanket that surrounds Earth.

This condition might cause global temperatures to rise by several degrees over the next 50 years. Indeed, the warming trend might be sufficient to melt a large portion of the polar ice caps and cause sea levels to rise. The trend could cause tropical conditions to move northward in the Northern Hemisphere and southward in the Southern Hemisphere. The temperate zones would become warmer. Agricultural conditions would change around the world.

Such temperature variations due to carbon dioxide buildup can occur as a consequence of burning oil and coal, which are fossil fuels. Fossil fuels are the residue of plants and animals that died millions of years ago. Coal is mainly a by-product of long-dead plant matter. When the plants died, their remains were gradually buried deeper and deeper by layers of earth. Plants are composed mainly of carbon compounds, and the pressure of the overlying earth slowly compressed the carbon into coal. Although some coal contains both carbon and impurities, hard coal is almost pure carbon. Carbon is inflammable and burns with a very hot flame. Burning coal releases CO_2 into the atmosphere.

Another fuel for the production of electricity is oil. Oil, too, is a fossil fuel. It comes from the remains of dead microscopic creatures that were buried under layers of earth. Oil is not a solid like coal, but a liquid form of carbon. Oil is the raw material from which gasoline is made. Burning oil and gasoline also releases CO_2.

Some atmospheric carbon dioxide is absorbed by green plants. However, most is dissolved into the water of the oceans. A small part of that carbon dioxide is used by sea creatures. They combine it with calcium to manufacture calcium carbonate. The sea creatures use the calcium carbonate to form their shells. Later, these shells fall to the sea floor. Thus, the activity of some of these small animals captures a minor portion of atmospheric carbon dioxide and retains it for very long periods of time.

In recent years, the production of carbon dioxide has outstripped the absorption capabilities of the seas, the sea animals, and the green plants. The portion of carbon dioxide that is not absorbed is retained in the atmosphere.

Climate Cycles

The climate of the Earth has changed many times in its 4.5-billion-year life span. The positions of the continents have also changed during that time. In the past 400 million years, the continents have come together in a single mass and then separated at least twice. As these landmasses have shifted over the surface of the Earth, they have passed through different climate zones. Scientists have found evidence that the frozen wastes of Antarctica were once a green and pleasant place.

Louis Agassiz, a Swiss-American naturalist, was one of the first scientists to study long-term changes in climate. In 1836, he noted the positions and markings on many large rocks found in the lower Alpine valleys of Switzerland. A few decades earlier, two Swiss scientists had noted that these boulders were identical to rocks embedded in high Alpine glaciers. Agassiz deduced that earlier glaciers had carried the rocks to the lower parts of the valleys. He also noted that the bedrock in valleys and on the lower slopes of mountains was marked with many parallel grooves. From these and other observations, Agassiz reasoned that in times past, the Swiss glaciers had been much larger.

Agassiz observed similar features in stretches of rock found in northern Europe and England. He came to believe that an ice sheet had once covered a large portion of the European continent. Most scientists were at first skeptical of his ideas. However, scholars from all over Europe were soon convinced by Agassiz's careful investigations and his excellent reputation. The following year, he expanded this theory. He proposed the existence of an ice age during which ice sheets had extended over northern Europe, Asia, and North America. This theory was too fantastic for his fellow scientists, and they laughed at his ideas. Nevertheless, Agassiz continued his research. He pointed out that the grooves in the areas of flat rock were parallel, continued for many yards, and were all oriented in a north-south direction. Agassiz believed that the deep cuts were made by stones carried along by the glaciers as they flowed over the bedrock. He also pointed out that mounds of dirt and stones were piled up where the grooves stopped. Agassiz reasoned that the glaciers had acted like bulldozers and pushed along debris to the farthest reaches of the ice sheets. Eventually, enough evidence accumulated to prove Agassiz's theory of extensive glaciation. By 1845, most scientists had accepted the concept of an ice age.

Louis Agassiz went on to become one of the most renowned naturalists in the history of science. In 1846, he visited the United States. The following year, Agassiz joined the science faculty at Harvard College (now University) in Cambridge, Massachusetts. He explored much of North and South America and recorded his observations of plants, fish, and animals. Agassiz was the moving force behind the establishment of the National Academy of Sciences in 1863.

New Forces in Climate Change

The transition period between cold and warm climate cycles generally covers several hundred years. However, humans are now confronted with the possibility that a serious climate change might take place in only a few decades. If so, major adjustments in agriculture, fishing, and forestry will be required.

The prospect of rapid climatic changes is the direct result of human activities. In the recent past, many people were totally unaware that their actions could prove destructive to the environment. People burned many things—coal, trash, leaves, and garbage—to heat their homes, cook their food, and keep their cities and farms free from debris. Not many years ago, children enjoyed the autumn treat of roasting marshmallows over a bonfire made from fallen leaves. No one thought that these activities would damage the atmosphere. Now, almost everyone knows that many of these activities are harmful. However, not everyone has been willing to change their behavior. People persist in following their past habits. For example, to save time and money, some factory owners continue to allow noxious gases to pollute the air. Because of these behaviors—whether innocent, thoughtless, or intentional—humans may be forced to make adjustments in the way they obtain food, clothing, and shelter in the near future.

2
The Weather

In England, people say, "If you don't like the weather, just wait a few minutes and it will change." Daily or even hourly change in the weather is a feature of the temperate zones. Some of these weather changes cause moderate discomfort. Cold rain is chilling, and wind makes it chillier. However, these conditions are not disastrous, and people can usually cope with them. For example, most people in England carry an umbrella if they plan to be outside for any length of time. On the other hand, some weather—snow, hail, or fog—produces dangerous conditions. Driving a car or just walking is hazardous. Growing crops can be flattened by hail. Major storms, hurricanes, and tornadoes destroy property and can cause fatalities for humans and animals.

Early Weather Prediction

At the dawn of history, weather was associated with religion. Ancient people looked to the gods for an explanation of the lightning and thunder generated by violent storms. Zeus, the "father" of the Greek gods, was originally a sky and weather god. He is often shown holding a bolt of lightning.

Weather prediction was based in part on superstitions. Human beings saw the flight of birds or the agitation of barnyard animals as forecasts of the gods' weather plans. Many people thought they could predict an unusually cold winter by the thickness of an onion skin or the density of a sheep's wool.

Although daily weather patterns were difficult to discern, seasonal changes did show a predictable pattern. This pattern was correlated by ancient observers with the heavenly locations of constellations and planets. Weather science began when these patterns were recorded and used for systematic predictions.

The ancients regarded the celestial changes as calendars and fixed their annual ceremonies by the heavenly configurations. Stonehenge, a circular monument of huge stones on Salisbury Plain in England, is thought to have been associated with one of the most famous seasonal rituals, the spring equinox celebration. The placement of the stones is correlated to the position of the Sun at the onset of spring.

Egyptian astronomers were the first to establish a one-year calendar of 365 days. Their calendar was probably based on observations of two very special events. These events happened each year within a few hours of each other. At dawn on the day that the Nile usually overflowed its banks, the Sun ascended into the sky, accompanied by the Dog Star, Sirius. The yearly flooding of the Nile brought precious water and new soil to the lands along the river and was vital to Egypt's agriculture. Therefore, the yearly cycle of life began with this event.

The early Greeks saw other weather patterns. They remarked on the connection between wind direction and temperature. About 350 B.C., the Greek philosopher Aristotle sought to study weather in a systematic manner. He observed that warm, moisture-laden air rose upward and formed clouds when it reached a high altitude. Aristotle's study of clouds, stars, planets, and other heavenly bodies led to his book *Meteorologica,* the study of "things above." Meteorology, the modern name of weather science, is based on this Greek word.

In the hundreds of years between Aristotle's time and the beginning of the 20th century, weather study and weather pre-

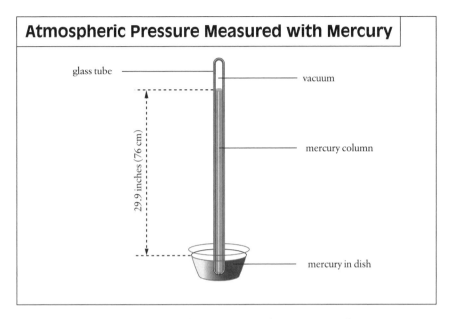

Atmospheric Pressure Measured with Mercury

glass tube

vacuum

29.9 inches (76 cm)

mercury column

mercury in dish

Atmospheric pressure pushes the mercury column 29.9 inches (76 cm) above the surface of the mercury in the dish. The column of mercury will climb slightly higher or fall slightly lower when the weather changes.

diction remained at the level of folk knowledge. Some of this lore was helpful for the farmers and sailors who depended on the weather. Keen observers could read cloud patterns and make fairly accurate, short-range predictions. Halos around the Sun or the Moon were reasonable indicators of coming storms. "Red sky in morning, sailor take warning—red sky at night, sailor's delight" is not a bad guide to a day's upcoming weather.

In the 1500s and 1600s, European scholars began to make significant improvements in weather science. Around 1500, during the High Renaissance, Leonardo da Vinci, an Italian artist and scientist, constructed a superior weather vane. Galileo, a famous Italian astronomer, invented the thermometer in 1593. His student Evangelista Torricelli made an instrument for measuring air pressure in 1643. This device later evolved into the modern barometer.

In 1653, Ferdinand II, grand duke of Tuscany, established several weather-recording stations in the area north of Rome. This project was the first to prove that similar weather patterns occurred in different locations at the same time. The duke also investigated the possibility that weather conditions in one location could be used to predict conditions at other locations.

In the early 1660s, Robert Boyle, an English chemist, began to study the physical nature of gases such as air. He was the first to show the relationship between pressure and the volume of a gas. He showed that air could be compressed and that it could also be removed from a container to make a near vacuum.

Around 1800, the French physicist Jacques Charles established the relationship between the compression of a gas and its temperature. His investigations began in 1783 while using hydrogen balloons to test the possibilities of human flight. His theory states that a gas becomes warm when compressed under pressure and cools after the pressure is released and the gas is allowed to expand.

The work of these scientists resulted in a series of studies that led to the belief that weather was the result of physical laws. If the belief were true, accurate weather predictions would be possible. Scientists hoped that meteorology would become an exact science by applying the proper physical laws to accurate measurements of temperature, wind speed, rainfall, and other variables. They were disappointed by the actual turn of events.

Forecasting

The British, French, and Spanish colonists who occupied North America in the 1600s were shocked by the violence of the winters. The eastern seaboard of North America—where most of these western Europeans settled—has a "continental climate." That is, the weather conditions experienced on the east coast develop over dry land to the west and are borne eastward by the prevailing winds. In contrast, European weather develops over the Atlantic Ocean and is affected by the mass of warm water carried by the current called the Gulf Stream to the northeastern Atlantic Ocean.

The Gulf Stream gets its warmth and its name from the Gulf of Mexico, where it originates. It carries warm water from the tropics along a path that is parallel to the east coast of the United States. Then it cuts across the Atlantic to the west coast of Europe where it disperses. Because of the presence of warm water off the west coast of Europe, those coastal regions have a warmer winter than the northeastern United States. Parts of eastern Europe, such as Poland and Russia—far from the warm Gulf Stream—experience the same harsh winter weather conditions as eastern North America.

By the late 1700s, observing weather conditions was a favorite hobby of prosperous Americans. George Washington, Thomas Jefferson, and Benjamin Franklin were avid weather watchers. They routinely recorded their observations of temperature, precipitation, wind conditions, and barometric pressure. George Washington made such notations on the day before he died in 1799.

Benjamin Franklin was involved in more active investigations of weather conditions. During a thunderstorm in 1751, he tied a key to a kite string. The position of the string allowed the key to touch the ground. He then flew the kite into the high wind of a thunderstorm. When a bolt of lightning struck the kite, the lightning traveled down the wet string. The string acted like a wire to conduct the electricity through the key into the ground. Franklin had shown that lightning and electricity were the same phenomenon. He survived his foolhardy investigation, but other men were electrocuted when they tried to duplicate his experiment.

In those colonial days, the scientific aspects of weather investigation were incorporated into a broad area of learning called natural history. Later, during the mid-1800s when scientific studies became more specialized, the field of meteorology was classified as a physical science. Much of the research, however, was in the hands of talented amateurs.

William Redfield, a prosperous New Yorker, studied meteorology as a hobby. Redfield examined weather charts that had been compiled over several years. He discovered that weather systems have both a circular movement and a curving, sideways movement. The circular movement accounts for wind direction, while the sideways movement indicates the direction

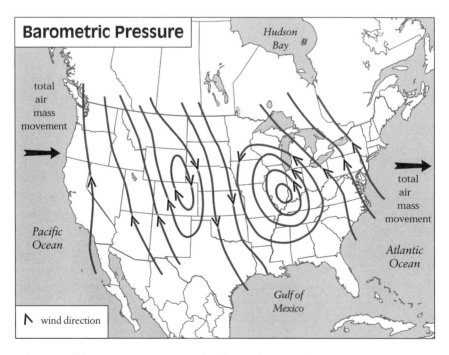

The curved lines connect points that have the same barometric pressure. The succession of lows and highs moves gradually from west to east across the continent.

in which the weather system is moving. If one knew the characteristics of the particular weather system, one could predict the effects along its path. Unfortunately, there was almost no communication between amateur meteorologists such as Redfield and the astronomers and technicians who tried to forecast the weather. Redfield's important discoveries received little attention at the time.

In the early 1800s, the U.S. government did not sponsor weather research. Politicians had little interest in scientists who theorized about the weather. They understood, however, the economic importance of being able to warn farmers and fishers of impending storms. Nevertheless, politicians were hesitant about spending money on weather research.

Although forecasters had few solid scientific theories or systematic observations at that time, they recognized that weather conditions in the United States usually originate in the west and travel toward the east. Even if weather information had been more scientific, weather forecasting would have improved very little. At the time, there were no fast communication systems to carry the weather observations.

The problem was partly resolved in 1832 when Samuel F. B. Morse, an American artist and inventor, filed a patent for the telegraph. Wires soon linked railroad stations and post offices from the Midwest across the Allegheny Mountains and on to Washington, D.C.

Joseph Henry, the first secretary (chief executive) of the Smithsonian Institution, used this technological advance to support a systematic weather service. By 1860, he had recruited 500 volunteers from various locations between Washington, D.C., and the Mississippi River. Every day, these volunteers used the telegraph to report weather observations to an office at the Smithsonian. The information was summarized, forecasts were composed, and the predictions were reported in the evening newspapers. Unfortunately, people whose work was most affected by the weather—farmers and

Joseph Henry was the first secretary of the Smithsonian Institution. He attempted to establish a weather-reporting system manned by volunteers, but his work was interrupted by the outbreak of the Civil War. (Courtesy of the National Oceanic and Atmospheric Organization)

sailors—did not have access to the newspapers. Communities near Washington, D.C., tried several methods to speed the flow of information. Their systems, such as raising signal flags on the roofs of post offices, were not very successful. Although Henry's concept was a step in the right direction, the predictions were not very accurate. The outbreak of the Civil War disrupted his system, and it was shut down in 1863.

Military operations during the Civil War demonstrated that weather information could be a valuable asset to commanders in the field. Consequently, after the war ended, former military men elected to the House of Representatives worked to establish a new weather service. They wanted the service to be a part of the government so that it could not be interrupted by the decisions and varied dispositions of private individuals.

In 1870, President Ulysses S. Grant, a former army general, approved a congressional resolution to found a national weather service. Grant directed the U.S. Army to create the organization. Because weather reports were carried by telegraphy, the first national weather service was assigned to the army's Signal Corps. There were soon 24 weather observation stations on military bases around the country.

Although the service was operated by military personnel, civilian scientists were employed as expert consultants. In

1871, a young physicist, Cleveland Abbe, was appointed to be the civilian special assistant to the commander of the Signal Corps. His appointment led to gradual improvements in weather observation, reporting, and forecasting.

Abbe was typical of the weather scientists of the time. His basic training was in astronomy and physics. After graduating from a New York college, Abbe did postgraduate work at the University of Michigan with a visiting German astronomer, F. F. E. Brunnow. He then worked as a research assistant to Professor B. A. Gould. Gould was on leave from the University of Michigan and working for the U.S. government at the U.S. Coastal Survey office in Cambridge, Massachusetts. There, Abbe became aware of the strong interdependence of weather

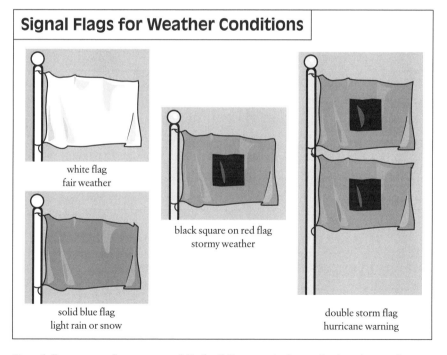

Signal Flags for Weather Conditions

white flag
fair weather

black square on red flag
stormy weather

solid blue flag
light rain or snow

double storm flag
hurricane warning

Signal flags were flown on public buildings to inform the local populace of upcoming weather conditions.

science and the practical work of weather prediction. While preparing the publication of the *Nautical Almanac* at the survey office, he saw that scientists involved in scholarly research were also working on projects to support sailors and fishers. He saw that scientists were gaining new ideas from these studies and from the procedures used by the weather forecasters.

After his eye-opening experiences in New England, Abbe traveled to Russia for two more years of postgraduate study in astronomy. There he found the same spirit of collaboration between scientists and weather forecasters. This collaboration was uncommon in western Europe and the eastern United States. It was a lucky accident that Abbe experienced this cooperation in two successive settings.

When he returned to the United States, Abbe attempted to establish an astronomical observatory in New York that would be similar to the Russian model. However, his efforts collapsed, and he took a position with an established observatory in Cincinnati, Ohio. After two years in Cincinnati, Abbe became a consultant to the newly formed Weather Service of the U.S. Signal Corps.

Abbe sought to expand Joseph Henry's ideas by increasing the number of stations that would record weather information. By 1878, he had established 254 observation stations, which reported to the Weather Service three times each day. The information covered temperature, barometric pressure, relative humidity, wind information, cloud cover, and precipitation. By 1888, each station made nine reports a day. Two-day weather predictions reached a new level of accuracy. The reports became more reliable in anticipating major storms that could threaten lives, damage crops, and endanger ships on the Great Lakes or near the Atlantic coast.

In 1890, the Weather Service was transferred from the U.S. Army to the Department of Agriculture and the name was changed to the U.S. Weather Bureau. Shortly afterward, Abbe and others in the new bureau recognized the need to gather

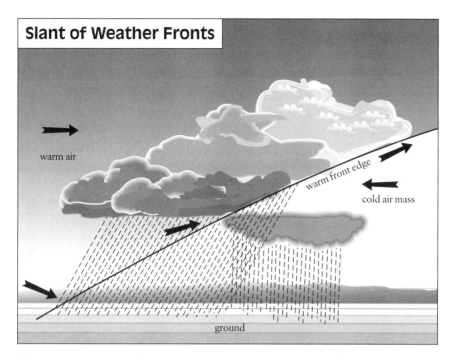

Slant of Weather Fronts

warm air

warm front edge

cold air mass

ground

When meteorologists learned to measure temperature with instruments on kites or balloons, they realized that weather fronts were slanted rather than straight up and down.

information about conditions in the air above the surface of the Earth. Studies of the upper layers of air are known as the "third dimension" in weather science. Meteorologists recognized that conditions in the third dimension are often different from those on the surface. For example, clouds on high can sometimes be seen to move in a different direction than surface winds.

At first, high-altitude information was gathered by weather instruments carried aloft by large box kites. However, kites could not reach altitudes high enough to satisfy the weather analysts. In 1909, scientists began investigating the use of balloons, manned aircraft, and even dirigibles to gather high-altitude information. The studies soon showed consistent weather patterns in the third dimension. For example, when masses of cold and warm air meet, the heavier, cold air tends to advance in a wedge shape under the lighter, warm air.

When the cold air is moving, the boundary between the cold and warm air is called a cold front. When a warm air mass moves to meet a stationary cold mass, the cold air stays at ground level and forces the warm air to rise along its edge. This weather condition is called a warm front and often brings rain.

These early attempts to understand climates and the weather were made before any serious attention was given to air pollution. The early work paved the way for more refined studies of weather and climate conditions. Those more refined studies then provided the foundation for showing how atmospheric conditions contributed to pollution and how industrial gases react with the natural gases of the atmosphere.

3
Modern Meteorology

During the early 1900s, European meteorologists began to investigate the movement of the air in large weather systems. One of the major figures in these studies was Vilhelm Bjerknes. Vilhelm's father, Carl Anton Bjerknes, was a physicist who taught applied mathematics at the Royal Frederik University at Christiana (now Oslo), Norway. In the late 1800s, Carl Anton's research was concerned with the natural movements of one liquid in another liquid, such as ink in water.

Vilhelm served as his father's research assistant while he continued his schooling. After completing his doctoral studies in Norway and two years of postdoctoral work in Germany, Vilhelm accepted a lecturer's position at a private college in Stockholm, Sweden. His father was pleased. There, Vilhelm would be available to edit his father's research reports and combine the material into a book. However, by the time the book was finished, new ideas in physics had outdated much of the work.

While working on his father's book, Vilhelm continued his own research. Although he did not see the connection, other scientists saw that Vilhelm's research with liquid movements was applicable to the activity of turbulent masses of air. Bjerknes was not particularly interested in these technical applications because his interests were focused on gaining recognition for his father's work. He was aware, however, that most scholars expressed more enthusiasm about the practical applications of the research than they did about the theoretical aspects.

This photograph of a weather balloon–launching platform was taken about 1906. (Courtesy of the National Oceanic and Atmospheric Administration)

The Physics of Weather

Gradually, the younger Bjerknes was persuaded to work less on his father's manuscripts and more on projects to improve weather predictions. At first, Bjerknes looked upon the practical side of his work as a hobby rather than serious scientific investigation. He soon realized that the Scandinavian governments funded practical research on fisheries and farming but had no great interest in theoretical physics. Bjerknes also knew that his students found good jobs working to improve weather prediction. Several of his former students soon made more money than their professor.

After 1900, weather research was becoming more important in the larger countries of central Europe. Aviation had become a respectable activity and a focus of scientific and economic interest. The Zeppelin airship was accepted as a practical means to haul cargo through the sky. Powered balloons were flown around the Eiffel Tower in Paris. The interest in human flight created a new interdependence between humankind and weather. In addition, advances in aviation allowed high-altitude observations of air temperature, air pressure, and wind. These measurements were used in new weather forecasting, which made the skies safer for flying.

By 1902, Bjerknes became preoccupied with the prospect of making meteorology into an exact science. He reasoned that he was not abandoning pure science because meteorology was a branch of physics. At the time, his argument was unrealistic because meteorology was not yet a well-structured physical science. However, the belief allowed Bjerknes to cling to his, and his father's, ideals and contemplate new avenues of research.

In spring 1903, his father died. While this was a sad event, it freed Bjerknes from his father's work and allowed him to apply theoretical physics to weather prediction.

On a short lecture tour in the United States in 1905, Bjerknes met R. S. Woodward, president of the newly founded

Carnegie Institution in Washington, D.C. Woodward offered Bjerknes a research grant to support his studies of the atmosphere.

Bjerknes spent the next 12 years focused on standardizing methods to measure meteorological effects. For example, Bjerknes sought to standardize the measurements of barometric pressure. He also hoped to gain international agreement on techniques to chart such measurements in the form of synoptic weather maps. The term *synoptic* comes from the Greek for "seeing together" and refers to how these maps present a graphic depiction of weather information from many separate weather stations. Analysts used the information to predict future weather conditions. The early maps were difficult to use because forecasters employed a variety of symbols and notations in their graphic depictions. Bjerknes was responsible for standardizing synoptic weather maps, and his symbols are now employed around the world.

Weather predictions improved with the use of synoptic maps and because aviators began routinely reporting conditions aloft. However, many difficulties continued to exist. The number of weather stations was insufficient, and weather analysts experienced delays in receiving necessary information.

Because of his Carnegie grant, Bjerknes was able to leave his teaching job in Stockholm and return to Norway in 1907. He enjoyed living in his native country, but felt isolated from the rest of the scientific community. In 1912, after five years in Norway, Bjerknes accepted a professorship in Leipzig, Germany. The Germans had made great strides in aeronautics. They were confident that Bjerknes's research in weather science would help the field of aviation. After World War I broke out in 1914, Bjerknes remained for a time in Germany. In 1917, his government called him back to Norway to work on the practical problems of weather forecasting for farming and fishing enterprises. Norway was a neutral country during the war, and these businesses flourished because both sides in the conflict needed to import food. Consequently, the Norwegian govern-ment funded a strong program to improve weather forecasting.

Bjerknes and his colleagues set about establishing a network of observation stations and a method to speed the information to an analysis center. Many of the stations were west of Nor-way on ships anchored in the North Sea. Information from these western locations was invaluable because most storms came from that direction. The stations had to be situated at some distance from the west coast of Norway to allow weather analysts sufficient time to interpret and transmit vital informa-tion about approaching storms.

Transmitting the predictions continued to be a problem because the people who needed the information were scattered around the country. To improve the situation, Norway and the other Scandinavian countries invested heavily in telephone and telegraph systems during the last years of World War I and in the immediate postwar period.

Just as Vilhelm had supported his father's scientific efforts, Vilhelm's son, Jacob entered the field of scientific meteorology. However, this partnership was far happier than the previous one. Jacob had a special genius for interpreting weather maps, and the two men made great progress in accurate predictions. Their forecasts were aided by a new source of information. During the war, the British had restricted the transmission of weather information because the German enemy might benefit from the broadcasts. After the war, weather observations from the British Isles, situated farther west than the Norwegian weather stations, were made available to the meteorologists in Norway and other European countries.

Other British Developments

In Great Britain, Lewis Richardson, a mathematical physicist, was working on ideas similar to those of Bjerknes. Richardson was frustrated in his attempts to be recognized as a theorist and to obtain a faculty position at Cambridge University. He had been appointed to a series of industrial, academic, and government posts before joining the British government's Meteorological Office in 1913. Richardson used his mathematical skills to develop the first mathematical models of weather processes. The models describe, for example, the manner in which patches of relatively calm air can exist within larger storm systems. Richardson compared this air movement to the small whirlpools seen in a moving stream of water. Although the Englishman and the Norwegian did not, at first, know of each other's work, their ideas proved to be closely related.

After World War I began in 1914, the activities of the Meteorological Office were directed more and more to meet the needs of the British military services. Soon, Richardson became uncomfortable with the work. He was a pacifist because of his religious upbringing as a Quaker (a member of the Society of Friends). Richardson resigned his job and joined a Quaker ambulance unit attached to the French army. Later in his life, Richardson analyzed international conflicts and studied methods to resolve such conflicts by peaceful means.

Modern Tools

New ideas, techniques, and advanced instrumentation followed the pioneering work of Bjerknes and Richardson. Modern weather forecasting progressed to the stage where seven-day forecasts are possible. Major hurricanes are tracked from their origins in the Atlantic Ocean or the Gulf of Mexico. Affected coastal areas are given hours and even days of advance warning. Citrus growers in Florida are alerted if frost is coming. Beachgoers in New Jersey are cautioned when the bright sunshine could cause sunburn.

Weather forecasts shown on television are the result of 50 years of extraordinary advances in weather science. A bird's eye view of weather patterns—such as looking down into the eye of a hurricane—is one of the most dramatic visual presentations. Other newspaper and television images are equally spectacular. A single picture can now represent weather conditions on an entire continent. Enormous quantities of information can be summarized by the use of color graphics. Television weather forecasters can show cloud formations moving across large areas of the United States. Moreover, the movements of clouds and storms over a 24-hour period can be presented by speeded-up, graphic animation. Weather information is now understandable to everyone.

These presentations are based on three technical advances: orbital satellites, radar, and high-speed digital computers. Orbital satellites carry cameras and other instruments high above the surface of the Earth. Some of these satellites circle the Earth from north to south and cross over the Arctic and Antarctic regions in each orbit. Other satellites, in much higher orbits, remain permanently stationed over one area. These are called geostationary satellites. Both types of satellites take digital photographs of the weather activity below them. The information is sent to ground stations by special electronic communication links. These pictures greatly expand the information supplied by weather stations on the ground and provide new perspectives for weather analysts.

Radar provides another major advance in the assembly of information. Radar sends out electronic signals that are reflected by objects in the air or on the ground. The reflected signal pattern is detected by an antenna and relayed to a special television tube. The patterns are interpreted by a professional meteorologist. Early radars could detect only solid objects, but the newer radars obtain reflections from falling rain and even from clouds. The best ground-based radars can discern small areas of intense turbulence that could easily escape detection by satellites. These technological advances help meteorologists to record thousands of observations over extended periods of time.

Modern computers allow the integration of such weather information into a single, highly meaningful representation. The computers have been programmed to perform specific mathematical operations on the data supplied by satellites, radars, and other standard weather instruments. The computer programs are based partly on the mathematical models first conceived by Bjerknes and Richardson. These computer mod-

Personnel who fly into hurricanes to determine their composition and dynamics are known as "stormhunters." In 1966, this crew tried to break up a hurricane by dispersing silver iodide crystals. Project Storm Fury, as the attempt was called, was not successful. (Courtesy of the National Oceanic and Atmospheric Administration)

els are vastly improved. For example, a computer can be programmed to draw weather maps.

Without these capabilities for understanding the hourly movement of air masses and the long-term cycles of climate, it would not be possible to grasp the effects of air pollution.

4

Advances in Weather Studies

One hundred and fifty years ago, government scientists established a handful of weather stations. By using the newly developed telegraph system, the scientists were able to obtain sketchy meteorological information two or three times a day. By 2005, the National Weather Service (NWS) maintained more than 1,500 automated, land-based weather stations, hundreds of anchored, weather buoys, and dozens of unanchored weather buoys that float in the oceans and the Gulf of Mexico. In addition, 50 lighthouses have been augmented with modern equipment and serve as automated weather stations. All the stations report their weather data every 30 minutes to information processing centers.

In addition, raw weather data is fed into the centers from some 6,000 volunteer-manned weather observation sites. Some of these sites are located on college and university campuses, where science students oversee the operations as part of their learning program. Many more stations are operated in school settings by elementary, middle, and high school students. Manning the school-sponsored stations allows students to combine learning experiences with an interest in amateur meteorology. This volunteer program is called "Weather Bugs" and is sponsored jointly by the NWS and a commercial vendor of weather instruments. The Weather Bugs are responsible for alerting local police and fire-and-rescue units during emergencies, such as chemical spills, where weather conditions are likely to play an important role. The service, endorsed by the Department of Homeland Security, also helps with local problems such as gas pipeline leaks and brush fires.

While the NWS has a good reputation for providing the public with timely warnings of impending disasters, the Indian Ocean tsunami of December 26, 2004, has raised questions about the breadth of NWS services. Tsunamis are giant waves caused by underwater earthquakes and volcanic eruptions. Technically, tsunamis are geophysical and not meteorological events and therefore are outside the normal scope of NWS

The DART buoy is linked to an underwater pressure gauge that activates a warning signal when a tsunami wave passes. (Courtesy of the National Oceanographic and Atmospheric Administration)

responsibilities. Nevertheless, the National Oceanographic and Atmospheric Administration (NOAA) and the NWS do maintain a tsunami warning system in the Pacific Ocean. However, the beneficiaries are American or South American residents. Unfortunately, no one maintains any tsunami detectors in the Indian Ocean. One reason for the lack of detectors is in the nature of the threat. Historical reviews of tsunami events suggest that the threat is small. Thus, while there have been many earthquakes in countries facing the Pacific and Indian Oceans, most are inland and do not cause tsunamis. Those that occur underwater are normally not very strong and typically generate waves only six to nine feet in height that cause only moderate damage. On average, about two of these small to moderate tsunamis occur every year.

In 1964, however, a major earthquake took place off the Aleutian Islands that extend westward from Alaska. The resulting tsunami caused 106 deaths in Alaska and 11 more as far away as Crescent City, California. In 1975, an earthquake in the Pacific near Hawaii generated waves of over 24 feet (7.6 m) and caused two people to lose their lives. In 1996, an earthquake off the coast of Peru generated waves reaching 90 feet (30 m) that destroyed the Peruvian villages of Rio Santas and Coishco and caused 12 deaths. The Sumatran tsunami of December 26, 2004, dwarfed these earlier disasters with its death toll above 100,000 and has led to a revision of the perception of the threat. World leaders now see the advantage of a worldwide network of tsunami detectors and a more comprehensive warning system.

NOAA's detectors are called DART (Deep-ocean Assessment and Reporting of Tsunamis). The key element in the DART system is a pressure gauge that is anchored to the ocean bottom at a depth of 30,000 feet (10 km). A buoy is stationed on the surface just above the pressure gauge. As a wave builds up, the activity causes a momentary change in the weight of water above the gauge. When such a pressure change is detected, the information is sent by sound signals to a receiver on the buoy. In turn, signals are transmitted by radio to a communications satellite that relays the warning to a NWS center.

By 2004, six DART systems were in place in the Pacific Ocean. Three are placed south of the Aleutian Islands, about 2,000–3,000 miles (3,200–4,600 km) west of the Alaskan mainland. Two are west of the Washington-Oregon coast and one is in the South Pacific off the coast of Chile. Each system is stationed sufficiently far from the nearest shore so that residents can receive warnings at least eight or 10 hours before the expected event. Such an arrangement is analogous to the tornado warnings given to residents of the south-central and eastern United States. Both systems are intended to allow sufficient time for an orderly evacuation of the threatened area.

There appear to be two lessons that can be learned from the tragedy. First, the public service functions of geophysics and meteorology should be more closely coordinated. The very large earthquake (nine plus on the Richter scale—a near record) that caused the tsunami was detected by seismographs in the region. These earthquake detections could have provided the basis for a tsunami warning. Second, the warning messages must be transmitted over effective communication channels to reach potential victims.

Some remedial actions are already underway. For example, the United States is supporting an international effort to develop an integrated Earth observation system called GEOSS

Weather buoys are automated, floating weather stations. They are deployed and maintained by specialists aboard weather ships. The meteorological data taken in by the instruments on the buoy are relayed via satellite to central computers. (Courtesy of the National Weather Service)

(Global Earth Observation System of Systems). Among other concrete steps, NOAA will install 32 new DART buoys in the Pacific and Atlantic Oceans by mid-2007.

Meteorologists also hope that new observational techniques can give an even longer warning period. The series of high waves sometimes signals its presence by causing choppy ripples to form at the front edge of the tsunami. The ripples make a darker than normal band or stripe in the water. Soon, satellite radar may be able to detect the darkened stripe while the tsunami is still far from the nearest coast. The warning period could then be extended and the evacuation of people could proceed at a more orderly pace.

Weather information is also collected on the surface of the ocean from both anchored buoys and those allowed to drift free with the water currents. The National Weather Service also operates two weather ships that are deployed at sea for about 10 months of each year. In addition, weather information is collected voluntarily by crew members on more than 4,000 merchant ships and relayed by radio to NWS centers at least four times a day—more often when severe conditions are present. The World Meteorological Organization, part of the United Nations, supports this important program of information collection.

On land, variations in water levels pose particular challenges for the National Weather Service. Specifically, both flood and drought conditions have serious economic and safety consequences. The U.S. Department of Agriculture (USDA), the U.S. Geological Survey, the U.S. Army Corps of Engineers, and the National Weather Service perform a flood and drought watch jointly. Under a current interagency agreement, the NWS now maintains and operates almost 3,000 river flow and depth gauge instruments in the United States, American Samoa, Guam, and Puerto Rico. A device similar to a wind gauge or weather vane measures flow rate. This device looks somewhat like an arrow with a small propeller substituted for the arrowhead. The flow gauge is connected to a post embedded in the

Ronald H. Brown, *the weather ship, is seen here off the coast of the Portuguese island of Madeira near the mid-Atlantic.* (Courtesy of the National Oceanic and Atmospheric Administration)

river bottom and held below the surface of the water. The water flow turns the propeller at a rate determined by the flow speed. Water depth is measured by the height of a float that is tethered to a vertical stake. All the information is recorded automatically by the instruments (which are housed in small, wire structures) and then relayed to a prediction center. Information about both stream depth and flow rate is necessary to make adequate judgments about the condition of the stream.

Regular measurements of soil moisture would be a great help in determining the possibility of drought conditions. Unfortunately, no systematic soil moisture-sampling program is in place. However, the information about stream levels, flow rates, rainfall amounts, relative humidity, and soil types are now interrelated to generate reasonable approximations of actual soil moisture. The USDA leads the effort to project drought predictions in collaboration with the World Agricultural Outlook Board of the U.S. Commerce Department. This effort is also linked to the United Nations through the World Meteorological Organization and the Food and Agriculture Organization. While it is not possible to prevent droughts, officials hope to moderate the adverse effects by careful management of programs such as irrigation and water storage.

To obtain weather information from above the Earth's surface, the NWS uses a system of untethered balloons. Two balloons are launched every day from 92 sites in the United States. The balloons typically rise to 20 miles (32 km) above the surface and collect information on temperature, humidity, wind direction, and atmospheric pressure at successive atmospheric layers. This data is immediately radioed back to a ground station. The balloons burst after reaching their maximum altitude and the instruments—enclosed in pre-addressed containers—descend by parachute. About 20 percent of the instruments are found and returned for repair and reuse.

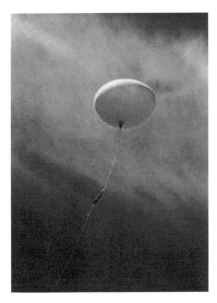

The parachute that will soften the fall of the instrument package after the balloon bursts in the stratosphere is visible on the tether below the balloon. (Courtesy of the National Weather Service)

The crews of commercial and private aircraft—like the crews of merchant ships—provide a voluntary reporting service. The members of the Aircraft Owners and Pilots Association work in cooperation with NWS specialists to record weather conditions—particularly storms aloft, dangerous air turbulence, and wind shear effects. The participation of pilots in weather reporting is a tradition carried over from the early days of aviation, when such information was less centralized and less reliable. In those days, pilots readily recognized that observations by other pilots could be lifesaving. A quick radio message from one pilot to another or to a dispatcher would warn of dangerous conditions. Now, such verbal exchanges are managed by a NWS center in Kansas City, Missouri. This center also routinely receives reports from automated stations located at hundreds of airports around the country.

The most glamorous advances in meteorology have been made in instrumentation—particularly the instruments found in orbiting space satellites. The NWS now operates two types of advanced satellites. One type of satellite uses a high-altitude synchronous system—a system in which the orbital speed of the satellite is matched with that of the Earth's rotation and therefore remains over the same geographical position. The other type is called a polar orbiter. This satellite flies at a lower altitude and orbits in a north-south path.

The two active synchronous satellites called Geostationary Operational Environmental Satellite (GOES) maintain a fixed position above the equator. One GOES is positioned over the Pacific Ocean and can view much of North America. The other is positioned over Central America with a view of central and eastern North America as well as all of South America. The two fields of view overlap so that all of North America is covered. In fact, the two satellites together see 60 percent of the Earth's surface. The viewing of this large area, which is scanned in less than 30 seconds, is possible because the satellites are in very high orbits—22,300 miles (35,000 km) above the surface.

GOES was developed and launched by the National Aeronautics and Space Administration (NASA). Once in orbit, the satellites were brought under the operational control of the

One of the two operational GOES satellites can detect weather conditions over an area that encompasses about 40 percent of the Earth's surface. (Courtesy of the National Aeronautics and Space Administration)

This picture of a polar orbiter after an accident on the production line shows the inner workings of the satellite. (Courtesy of the National Aeronautics and Space Administration)

National Oceanographic and Atmospheric Administration (NOAA), the parent organization of the National Weather Service.

The first prototypes of geosynchronous satellites were launched in the late 1960s. Since then, new capabilities have been added. Now the systems include two main viewing instruments: the "imager" and the "sounder." The imager records visible reflections from cloud formations, moisture density readings from a moisture sensitive wavelength, and infrared radiation from areas of elevated temperatures. The sounder measures moisture and heat at different altitudes.

The second type of satellite, the polar orbiter, flies a north-south path at a much lower altitude than GOES (at about 500 miles, or 850 km). As with GOES, there are two operational vehicles. Both have normal orbital periods of 24 hours. One crosses the equator at 7:30 A.M. ET each morning, and the other crosses the equator at 1:40 P.M. each afternoon. The polar orbiters have a smaller field of view than the geosynchronous satellites but provide much higher resolution when imaging cloud formations or the sources of elevated temperature.

Both types of satellites also function as astronomical observatories. The GOES monitors the flow of atomic particles traveling near the Earth, detects X-ray emissions from outer space, and records changes in the Earth's magnetic field. The polar orbiters detect the rate of protons—positively charged atomic particles—that flow from the Sun and the density of free electrons—negatively charged atomic particles.

The satellites also serve as communications relays. The polar orbiter, in particular, is tuned to receive distress signals from search-and-rescue beacons, small radio transmitters that can be attached to a life raft or vest carried by campers in a backpack. Both satellites relay data from stationary weather stations on the surface.

Mapmaking

Other important advancements in weather prediction have been made in the field of geodesy—the science and technology of measuring the Earth's surface. Accurate maps, the essential starting point of weather forecasting, are constructed from such measurements. The U.S. Coast and Geodetic Survey, the organization that provides the information for mapmaking, is part of the National Oceanographic and Atmospheric Administration (NOAA) and therefore has close ties to the National Weather Service.

One of the new tools of geodesy is the Global Positioning System (GPS), another system that depends on satellites. In this technology, each satellite acts as a message relay station or transponder. There are always 24 operational satellites in orbit and others are launched periodically so that defective vehicles can be replaced quickly.

The GPS can work with any number of ground stations. The actual number is unknown but is probably in the millions. For less than $100, anyone can own a workable, handheld version.

When the user activates the GPS monitor, a signal is sent to the three closest satellites. The minicomputer in the GPS monitor processes the incoming signals—sent back from the satellites—and the display almost immediately shows the exact geographical position of the monitor (and its user).

A valuable feature of the GPS is the ability to map exact surface details of an area. As suggested in the discussion of microclimates, ground features can influence the weather. On a large scale, the Appalachian Mountains serve as both a pathway and a barrier for weather masses. Low-pressure centers that originate in the Gulf States tend to swing to the northeast and follow the line of the Appalachian chain up to the coastal states. On the other hand, rainy weather coming east from the central states often seems to break up and diminish upon reaching the mountain barrier.

The GPS is also used to map gravity variations over large areas and surface fluctuations caused by the tidal pull of the Moon. The crust can rise and fall as much as one foot during a tidal cycle. Although gravity differences and crustal movements are tiny factors compared to variations in the weather, this information has been helpful in some areas. Earth scientists can now confirm the theory of continental drift. They have established that the yearly, tectonic movement of the Hawaiian Islands' crustal plate is exactly 2.66 inches (6.75 cm) to the northwest.

Consumers

Predictions and forecasts are derived from an extensive collection of meteorological information. Predictions are typically stated as a probability—a weatherperson might say that there is a 40 percent probability of rain tomorrow. Meteorologists are now able to funnel large volumes of numerical weather measurements through high-speed computers and arrive at such predictions. However, people who want to travel or engage in outdoor activities are not very happy with such statements. They want dependable forecasts. Forecasters depend on the information generated by supercomputer-based weather models, which are programmed to integrate the meteorological measurements sent by all the weather stations into a central place, the National Center for Environmental Prediction at Camp Springs, Maryland, a few miles southeast of Washington, D.C. After the computers have processed and incorporated this vast amount of data, scientists in the United States are given current and short-term weather predictions. The scientists integrate the computer-generated weather information and other sources of data—such as local radar images, their scientific training, and their expertise in dealing with weather conditions—to produce carefully scripted weather forecasts.

Weather Models

Jules Charney, a meteorologist, developed the first computer-based weather models in the late 1940s. His work was based on the mathematics developed before World War II by the English scientist Lewis Richardson. Charney prepared a large grid of the area being studied. Because computers at the time had very limited capabilities, the grid points were not close together (about 450 miles [720 km] apart). Altitude calculations were also restricted. These were confined to only one height—30,000 feet (9,144 m)—well above the surface of the Earth. The restrictions in area and altitude meant that the number of variables was left small so that early computers could process the computations.

Meteorological measurements were attached to the grid points, and the computer was instructed to process all the data and then move the weather conditions forward by 30 minutes. So, for example, if a storm over Seattle, Washington, was registered at the beginning of a 30-minute cycle, information about the storm, such as the prevailing winds and other factors, would be fed into the computer. The printout might show that storm would be over Tacoma, Washington, at the end of the 30-minute cycle. Charney's goal was to integrate a set of weather facts with rules of meteorological processes and be able to compute the weather changes that would evolve over a 24-hour period. This would constitute a one-day forecast. Unfortunately, the early computers were so slow that a whole day's worth of computing was required to run the model that would determine each day's forecast. Although these early models were clumsy and cranky, they demonstrated the possibilities of future computer forecasts. Now, the super-speed computers at Camp Springs can digest the whole world's data inputs and churn out weather results that represent up to 10-day projections.

As we have seen, there are two types of weather projections: forecasts and predictions. Human meteorologists with the aid of computer products and other information do forecasting. Weather predicting is the product of computer calculations. Most users of weather forecasts are primarily interested in local weather conditions. Consequently, a large portion of weather forecasting is handled by a decentralized system composed of 135 local Nation Weather Service (NWS) offices. Meteorologists that staff these offices have the benefit of computer-produced numerical predictions and large-scale national maps that carry images of such weather effects as infrared hot spots, the amount of moisture content at different altitudes, as well as the more standard patterns of atmospheric pressure. UNISYS, a private company under contract to NSW, records and condenses this national information on a composite

This geodesic radar housing protects the radar antenna. The whole system of which the housing and antenna are parts is called NEXRAD. The system incorporates the most advanced electronics and computer equipment. (Courtesy of the National Weather Service)

weather map. However, the official five-day local forecasts are the responsibility of local meteorologists.

Local newspapers and television stations serve as the principle users of these forecasts. In major metropolitan areas, the local TV station may control or have access to its own radar and computer-based conversion programs that generate multicolored images of developing weather events. The all-weather channel is the prime TV outlet. Since newspapers were for years the major source of weather forecasts for the public, it is noteworthy that the Weather Channel is owned and operated by the same company that owns a chain of newspapers.

Special Clients

The National Weather Service (NWS) has several clients among other government agencies. For example, the Aviation Weather Center in Kansas City, Missouri, is operated by the NWS in close collaboration with the Federal Aviation Agency (FAA). Raw weather data on conditions aloft is fed into the system from the NWS observation stations and weather balloons. In return, the FAA monitors and maintains in working order all the stations located at airports. The FAA also works with the Aircraft Owners and Pilots Association to coordinate reports of weather conditions that have been observed by private and commercial pilots.

The Department of Defense uses NWS information in conjunction with its own specialized weather capabilities. Military personnel maintain more than 100 weather stations located on military bases in the United States. They also maintain mobile weather stations and processing centers that can be deployed overseas.

Various government agencies have priority access to NWS data. The U.S. Forest Service (USFS) receives and processes all information about weather conditions that could affect forest fires. The U.S. Department of Agriculture (USDA) maintains a special office to receive all information concerning drought and flood prospects. This information is then relayed to all county extension agents and USDA employees so that farmers can be informed of threatening weather conditions. The farmers can then take appropriate steps to limit damage to crops and livestock.

In addition, the NWS has links to the World Meteorological Organization (WMO), a unit of the United Nations located in Geneva, Switzerland. A primary function of the WMO is to generate warnings of severe weather events for users of weather information around the world. Meteorological data from the United States is routed to Geneva through the National Climate Data Center in Asheville, North Carolina.

New Areas of Research

Mysterious lights in the sky have long been the subject of folktales. Weather scientists have also been fascinated by strange lights, such as the Aurora Borealis (Northern Lights). Many of these phenomena are now understood to be a consequence of the Sun's radioactivity. Other less dramatic lights have been noticed in recent years and are now being studied. These lights were previously ignored because their duration is short—only a fraction of a second. They were also disregarded because they appear above thunderclouds and come at the same time as more spectacular events such as intense lightning strikes. These phenomena are seen very high in the sky and appear as large blossoms of light. Atmospheric scientists have given them a fanciful name—"sprites."

Scientists now recognize that large electrostatic effects—events such as sprites that are the build up and discharge of electrical forces—occur in the atmosphere above the clouds. They now have detected even more mysterious occurrences. One is called the "blue jet." Blue jets are smaller than sprites—reaching from the cloud tops up to about 24 miles (40 km)—whereas sprites extend about twice as high. Another effect is called an "elf." This effect looks like a halo of light at altitudes of over 60 miles (100 km) and with a 30- to 40-mile (40- to 50-km) radius.

Scientists are now studying sprites, blue jets, and elves to determine the influence of such electrostatic events on local weather or global climate change. Sprites and other such electronic events that take place in the upper atmosphere may generate ozone. If so, scientists could be a little less worried about the dangerous effects brought about by ozone depletion.

5
Weather Modification

For thousands of years, humans have tried to influence the weather by songs, dances, and prayers to their gods. Shamans have presided over rituals to ensure good growing seasons. Today, people who live in rural societies are more attuned to the weather than those who live in cities. When news broadcasters announce that farmers are experiencing a drought, city dwellers merely feel they are enjoying another fine, dry, sunny day.

That people discuss the weather and complain about it but do nothing to change it is not exactly true. People have always controlled some aspects of their weather experiences. They have taken shelter in caves, tents, grass huts, and brick buildings from rain, snow, and hail. Even in primitive structures, a window, door, or other opening allows air circulation. A system of ventilation—no matter how crude—is a form of weather technology.

Microclimates

When humans wear clothing, they create a microclimate in the environment nearest their bodies. When they are inside a building, they experience two microclimates. The environment of the interior of the building differs from that of the exterior, and the conditions inside their garments differ from those outside the clothing.

Farmers are experts in establishing microclimates. In addition to providing a sheltered environment for their livestock, they shield their crops from adverse weather in several different ways. They provide wind breaks of dense shrubbery or trees to separate and protect their fields. They supply synthetic rain by the use of large sprinkler systems. In the citrus groves of California, Texas, and Florida, growers prevent frost from damaging the fruit by using water mists and artificial smoke to hold radiant heat near the ground.

Nature also produces microclimates. Coastal lands are part of a microclimate because the nearby water serves to moderate the weather. On the flat prairies of the Midwest, any rise in the contour of the land serves as a wind break, and conditions differ from one side of the hill to the other. However, some of the most dramatic microclimates are produced by human technology.

Every town and village has a climate that differs slightly from that of the surrounding countryside. In big cities, the differences in climate between city and nearby country can be

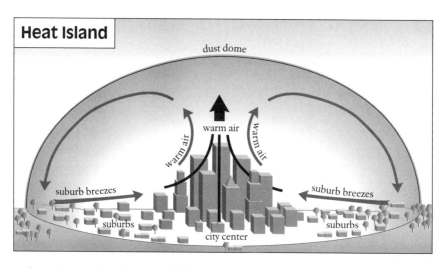

A densely populated area is likely to produce a heat island. Consequently, cities have a somewhat different climate from the surrounding countryside.

fairly large. Cities generate what are called heat islands. On hot summer days, asphalt streets and brick buildings absorb and retain heat from the Sun. At night, this heat is slowly radiated into the cooler air. Air conditioners transfer heat from the inside of a room or a building to the outside. All of a city's industrial processes generate surplus heat. In winter, buildings leak warm air from their heating systems and brick buildings absorb and then radiate any heat from the Sun. Snow seldom affects the core of a big northern city such as New York. The heat rising from the center of the city can melt the snow before or soon after it hits the ground.

Making Rain

The most important large-scale weather modification is the control of rainfall. In 1891, the secretary of agriculture—the cabinet member then in charge of the U.S. Weather Bureau—attempted to produce rain. He instructed his weather technicians to arm balloons with explosives and send them aloft. He hoped to generate rainfall by setting off the explosives when the balloons reached the clouds. C. W. Post, the founder of a major breakfast cereal company, tried similar experiments in 1911 and 1912. Fortunately, neither experiment was successful. Otherwise, explosions might have become a regular—and perhaps dangerous—response to every dry spell.

The first modern approach to rainmaking began in the 1930s. These early efforts were based on the way condensation occurs when warm, moisture-laden air is cooled quickly. The effects of condensation can be seen on a hot, muggy day when droplets of water form on a pitcher of iced lemonade. Scientists hoped that the same principle would apply if shaved ice were dropped into a moisture-laden cloud. The results were disappointing because no single aircraft could lift enough ice to make any impact on the clouds. Using a fleet of large aircraft would be too costly. In any case, shaved ice is an ineffective way of cooling the interior of a cloud. Indeed, the cloud's interior may contain cold air that is already below the freezing point of water.

Just before World War II, the development of high-altitude aircraft increased the knowledge of cloud structures. Scientists realized that the fine mist that makes up the body of the cloud can be very cold. German meteorologist Walter Findeisen theorized that rain occurs when the water in the cold mist condenses on solid particles and then freezes around them. When the frozen particles move through the cloud, they capture more water and grow larger and heavier. When they get heavy enough, they fall into warmer air, melt, and descend as rain. Findeisen decided that, in nature, the original starting particles were probably tiny ice crystals. In the language of weather science the crystals are called condensation nuclei—the nucleus or core on which the water condenses.

Findeisen wondered whether artificial crystals could be substituted for the naturally formed ones. He tried to seed clouds with condensation nuclei made of quartz and other materials, but the results were disappointing.

After the war, Vincent Schaefer and Irving Langmuir, a Nobel Prize winner in chemistry, began a program of meteorological research under the auspices of the General Electric Company. Langmuir had become interested in clouds from working on smoke-screen generators during the war. Schaefer was initially interested in the wonders of snowflakes and their near-perfect six-sided symmetry. Schaefer wanted to photograph individual snowflakes. He tried repeatedly to create the flakes from cold, moisture-laden air inside a refrigerator lined with black cloth. Nothing worked. One day, he forgot to close the refrigerator door when he took his lunch break. By the time he discovered his mistake, the refrigerator had warmed. Schaefer decided to use dry ice—frozen carbon dioxide—to correct the problem as quickly as possible. Dry ice is much colder than water ice, and it cooled the temperature of the refrigerator far below the freezing point of water. When Schaefer reopened the door and peered inside, his moist breath froze and became tiny ice crystals. Quite by accident, he had discovered that the extreme cold produced by dry ice could generate condensation nuclei from moist air.

Advanced Techniques

Experiments soon moved from the laboratory to the real world. Meteorologists demonstrated that condensation nuclei were produced when dry ice was released into clouds from an aircraft. These experiments verified Walter Findeisen's theory that the water carried by clouds condenses on crystals—either natural or artificial. Water then freezes on the nuclei, and the crystals grow larger and heavier, fall toward the Earth, and depending on temperature conditions, descend as rain, snow, or hail.

This weather-modifying technique was found to change the appearance of the rain clouds. Pilots conducting the tests reported that holes appeared in the clouds as soon as they were seeded with dry ice.

Further study showed that silver iodide crystals also could serve as condensation nuclei. When vaporized by intense heat, solid silver iodide breaks up into billions of tiny particles. The particles are almost weightless and resemble smoke or fog. The "smoke" of the vaporized silver iodide is so light that cloud seeding can be initiated from the ground. Wind currents can carry the "smoke" aloft and into the path of a prospective rain cloud. However, the most common seeding technique employs specially equipped aircraft to carry the silver iodide. No matter how the particles reach the clouds, each tiny sliver of silver iodide becomes the center of an ice crystal that eventually falls on the Earth as a form of precipitation.

Since the end of World War II, large-scale cloud seeding has become a commercial practice. In the United States, private companies are employed by county and state governments. The companies claim that they can increase rainfall by about 15 percent in a specific area during a given period of time. They also believe that cloud-seeding techniques can be used to prevent hail storms and to disperse fog. However, such claims are difficult to verify. Some of these weather changes may be the result of natural variations rather than human attempts at modification.

Some Reservations

Manipulating the weather can cause problems. When moisture-laden clouds are seeded to drop rain in a certain area, the clouds will be out of rain when they travel onward. The people in a dry locale might accuse the rainmakers of stealing their rain. If a group of farmers hires a company to cause rain on the same day as a local golf tournament, the golfers might be angry. Such cases have actually gone to court.

Government research on weather modification takes place at the National Center for Atmospheric Research in Boulder, Colorado. Scientists and technicians from this center have tested the most advanced techniques. For example, under an international agreement, special flares were tested in the desert areas of Mexico. These flares generate microscopic particles that act as condensation nuclei. Aircraft fly under thunderclouds and launch the flares upward into the clouds. The results have been encouraging. In some cases, this technique has increased rainfall about 30 percent over the normal amount.

However, many weather scientists argue that these conclusions may be based on wishful thinking. Specialists with no financial interest in weather modification suggest that seeding techniques produce an increase in rainfall of only 2 percent to 3 percent rather than 15 percent. They view these techniques as feeble, low-energy procedures that are too weak to upset the normal processes of a large rain cloud.

Scientific Shortfall

In 2001, the National Academy of Sciences convened a special panel on weather modification. The job of the panel was to determine the quality of the scientific research done to bring about an understanding of the basic principles of weather modification. The panel was also asked to review the successes and failures in weather modification activities in the field.

The panel made a public report in late 2003. The main finding was that very little basic research on weather modification had been done after the mid-1990s. By 2003, federal agencies were providing few funds to support such research. What little work was going forward was sponsored mainly by private sources or by academic departments in major universities. The lack of research meant that any attempts to evaluate current practices were severely limited. Nevertheless, sincere efforts to modify the weather were being initiated every year—primarily by state and local governments and private organizations. At least 66 such local projects were initiated in 2001. Similar efforts to change specific weather events were going forward in other countries. For example, provincial officials in northern sectors of China sponsored extensive cloud-seeding operations in 2004.

The Chinese projects were aimed at producing more rain for drought-stricken areas. However, activities in as many as 60 other countries were often focused on the modification of severe weather occurrences such as hail storms, hurricanes, and tornadoes. Only a few of such projects were subjected to rigorous scientific evaluation.

In 2004, the World Meteorological Organization (WMO) added its voice to the call for more basic research. In conjunction with the United Nations Environment Programme, the WMO suggested that a "roadmap" be prepared that would provide a long-range plan for basic research that could be supported by many countries acting together.

6

Local Air Pollution

Some air pollution comes from natural sources. Volcanoes can produce large quantities of toxic materials. Hot springs create modest amounts of noxious gases that contain the element sulfur. Forest fires caused by lightning generate air pollution. These fires produce some carbon dioxide, small amounts of toxic carbon monoxide, and oxides of nitrogen. Human activities, however, produce much larger amounts of these and other pollutants.

Early Cases

Fire is the most basic process underlying advanced technology. Fire is also the greatest contributor to air pollution. Since prehistoric times, fires kept people warm in winter, cooked food, lighted dark places, kept predators away, and hardened clay vessels. The earliest known fired clay pots were found in the Near East and dated around 7000 B.C. Fired vessels were used for cooking and for transporting and storing foods, liquids, or commodities. Their usefulness led to the technology of ceramics.

Fire is also used in the production of an important building material. For countless centuries, bricks were shaped from mud or clay and hardened in the sun. Around 3000 B.C., people in the Near East began to produce fire-hardened bricks. The molded clay was heated to a high temperature in a kiln or oven. Fire-hardened brick is a long-lasting and desirable building material.

The smelting or purification of metals is another ancient industry that requires the use of high temperatures. Small amounts of pure gold are found in riverbeds. Fire is not always necessary to purify gold. However, copper ore always contains sulfur or other foreign materials. Therefore, the ore must be purified by the use of intense heat. Archaeologists believe that copper was probably the first metal to be smelted. This industry may have begun in the Near East as early as 5500 B.C. and in Europe around 3500 B.C. Metals were smelted—melted from their ores—in primitive furnaces.

Usually, copper ore is found in the form of copper sulfate. When the ore is heated to the proper temperature, the sulfur is driven off as sulfur dioxide gas (SO_2) leaving the pure melted copper.

Although objects made from copper might be very beautiful, the sulfurous gases released by copper smelting are very unpleasant. A compound of sulfur and hydrogen has the same smell as rotten eggs and is disagreeable in even very small amounts. Gaseous compounds of oxygen and sulfur are far more dangerous because they can change to sulfuric acid in moist air. In those ancient times, copper smelting was a small-scale industry, but it may have been responsible for the first hazardous industrial pollutants. In fact, all ancient industries that required the use of fire were adding pollutants to the air.

In more recent times, the Industrial Revolution in Britain and northern Europe greatly increased metal-smelting operations. Smelting and other industries caused a dramatic increase in the quantity of pollutants sent into the atmosphere. Indeed, the amount of pollution has doubled every 10 years from the early 1800s to modern times.

Specific Effects

The Industrial Revolution took place in the years between 1750 and 1850. At that time, factories using newly developed complex machinery were hiring vast numbers of workers. People moved from farm communities to large cities to be near their jobs. The overcrowded cities were unable to cope with the new arrivals, and all areas of life were adversely affected. The industries were not regulated and had few rules regarding child labor, pollution, or the health and safety of workers. Unsafe gases and poisonous chemicals routinely escaped from the factories' smokestacks and pipes.

By the early 1800s, factories making lye and other caustic materials were sending especially toxic air pollutants into the atmosphere. These factories released hydrochloric acid gas in their smoke. It was soon apparent that the discharges were extremely harmful to the vegetation and buildings downwind of the factories. (The health of the workers inside the factories was not an issue.)

The British government eventually passed the Works Regulation Act of 1863. The act directed factory owners to remove hydrochloric acid from the smoke by passing it through large charcoal filters. This technique removed 95 percent of the acid. The owners found that the recovered hydrochloric acid was a valuable industrial product. Therefore, the law achieved a double benefit. The environment was protected, and the owners made money from the sale of the former waste material.

In the United States, early pollution problems were caused by large copper-, zinc-, and iron-smelting mills. Today, past environmental destruction is still visible in places where these metals were mined and processed over long periods of time.

In the mid- to late 1800s, steelmaking became a major industry in the United States. By 1900, the work was concentrated in locations such as Pittsburgh, Pennsylvania. Because steel production requires large amounts of both iron ore—the raw material of steel—and coal, these mills were built near centers of river and rail transportation. The iron ore was shipped in from Minnesota, and the coal was delivered from nearby coal mines. Although iron ore contains little sulfur, the coal used to heat the ore often has significant amounts of that element. The sulfurous gases sent into the atmosphere were devastating to growing plants. Many local farmers were ruined when the gases killed their crops.

During the mid-1800s, when industrialization was expanding rapidly through the United States, the government did little to regulate the industries. Protection from property damage and health hazards depended on local regulations and law courts. Politicians and judges knew that any attempt to regulate industrial activities could mean a loss of employment for the local citizens. The methods required to safeguard the atmosphere were costly, and when confronted, some owners simply moved their factories to different areas. Workers were given a choice. They could accept discomfort and health hazards, or they could lose their jobs. Similar situations still occur.

At that time, a lawsuit against the factory owners was the only way farmers could obtain compensation for the damage to their crops of livestock. If the farmer could prove that the factory was directly responsible for the loss, the local legal system would determine how much the factory owners should pay. However, few farmers had the money for a lawsuit. The offending industrial firm, on the other hand, usually could afford good defense lawyers. Not many individuals wanted to go into court unless they had strong evidence to support their cases.

As recently as the late 1940s, farmers in Tennessee complained that their crops and animals were being damaged by exposure to fluorine gas. The gas was being released during the purification of aluminum in some areas and during the production of phosphate fertilizers in others. The farmers' complaints resulted in a series of field studies conducted by the U.S.

Department of Agriculture. The findings from the field studies showed a correlation between the level of production at the industrial plants and the amount of damage to crops and live-stock. In 1951, the department sponsored a meeting of the interested parties in Washington, D.C. However, a direct causal link could not be proven by the correlation. The exchange of views between the farmers and the industrialists did little to resolve the problem. The farmers received no compensation because their claims were never settled.

The injustice of this situation eventually brought other federal agencies into the dispute. However, these officials were also reluctant to restrict industrial operations that provided employment and valuable products. Today, national and local governments seek a balance between the well-being of some individuals and the employment opportunities of others.

Smog as Local Pollution

Smog comes in two varieties: sulfurous and photochemical. Sulfurous smog began to appear at the height of the Industrial Revolution in the late 1800s. No one knows when photo-chemical smog first appeared in the atmosphere. However, scientists became concerned about this pollutant when automobile traffic expanded after World War II.

Smog is found mainly in or near large cities. Local weather conditions, local geography, and emissions from vehicles and factories all contribute to this dangerous form of pollution. Smog becomes most severe when the air is very calm and no wind disperses the polluting materials. Temperature inversions are particularly troublesome. Inversions occur when a warm mass of air sits atop a cooler, heavier air mass. If the cool mass lies in a valley or large low-lying area, the heavier air may not move for several days. Therefore, this stagnant air collects huge amounts of pollutants from industrial or automotive emissions or both. Los Angeles is famous for both terrible smog and long-lasting temperature inversions.

SULFUROUS SMOG

In 1905, an English public health official coined the word *smog* to describe a mixture of smoke and fog. In those times, the smoke from household coal fires contained significant amounts of sulfur dioxide and fine particles of sootlike materials. The water vapor (H_2O) in the foggy portion of the smog combined with the sulfur dioxide (SO_2) in the smoke to form sulfuric acid (H_2SO_4). This made the smog a serious health hazard.

Six years after coining the term, the same public health official announced that smog had claimed many lives in Edinburgh and Glasgow, Scotland. In 1930, sulfurous smog was thought to be responsible for 60 deaths in an industrial valley of Belgium. Twenty people died and hundreds were made ill in 1949 by a heavy smog in Donora, Pennsylvania. Four thousand fatalities were assigned to a four-day "killer" smog that struck London, England, in 1952.

Most of the victims were elderly people who suffered from chronic lung or heart problems. Those who wished to minimize the problem said that the smog may have shortened their lives but was not the sole cause of death. However, the evidence from long-term studies of air pollution strongly suggests that permanent damage to the lungs and circulatory systems builds up over time. This is true even when the pollution levels are relatively low. In any case, the evidence was sufficient to lead national governments to begin to restrict industrial emissions containing sulfur compounds.

For many years, burning coal was used to heat homes as well as generate electric power or smelt metal. At present, home heating is a minor source of sulfurous smoke. Electric power plants and other factories have continued to generate sulfur dioxide and other hazardous chemicals. Gradually, these companies realized that they must reduce the contamination caused by their pollutants. They developed better methods of combustion and waste disposal. The improved combustion yielded more heat from the same amount of fuel. The cleanup efforts produced additional benefits in the form of reclaimed, marketable materials. Consequently, improving the quality of air by reducing harmful emissions has a positive effect for both industry and the local communities.

PHOTOCHEMICAL SMOG

At present, photochemical smog is the more dangerous of the two smog hazards. Most photochemical smog is generated by materials released from automobile exhausts. The most prevalent pollutants include gaseous oxides of nitrogen, vapors from unburned gasoline, and fine particles of carbon-based compounds. When sunlight strikes these gases, ozone is formed by a complicated series of chemical reactions. Each molecule of ozone is composed of three atoms of oxygen (O_3). Therefore, ozone differs from life-giving oxygen molecules, which have two atoms of oxygen (O_2).

Ozone can cause stinging eyes and a raspy cough in anyone unlucky enough to be exposed to the gas. People who have chronic lung conditions or asthma are very vulnerable to ozone exposure. Such people are warned to limit their activities on smoggy days so that the bad effects will be minimized.

Photochemical smog becomes most dangerous when three conditions prevail. The first is heavy automobile traffic. The second is bright sunlight. The third is a stagnant air mass. Sometimes the air within a densely populated urban area generates a heat island. In such circumstances, the air tends to rise in the area of closely packed brick buildings and black-topped streets. The bricks and the tarred streets both absorb heat from the Sun and release it when the air cools. The warmed lighter

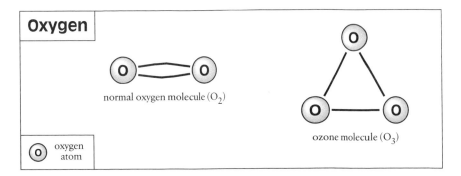

The common oxygen molecule has a double bond between its two oxygen atoms. Ozone has a single bond between each of three oxygen atoms. This structure makes ozone much more reactive than ordinary oxygen.

air ascends over the area, cools as it reaches a higher altitude, descends over the suburbs, and finally reenters the city. In other words, the same air circulates and recirculates within the city's boundary. During this time, pollution from automobile emissions and factories accumulates and becomes more and more concentrated.

A common factor in the generation of pollution is a temperature inversion, such as experienced by the city of Los Angeles, California, and other cities built in valleys or surrounded by hills. In the late 1940s and the 1950s, photochemical smog reached dangerous levels in Los Angeles. That city has very bright sunlight most of the year and unusually heavy automobile traffic. It is built on a very low-lying plain surrounded on three sides by mountain ranges. In short, Los Angeles provides all the critical conditions for smog production.

In the 1950s, the smog situation in Los Angeles was becoming intolerable. Smog alerts were broadcast on radio and television almost daily. Elderly people and those with lung problems were warned to restrict their activities. Infants were also vulnerable. Any active sport that caused rapid breathing was becoming risky. By 1954, experts recognized that exhaust products from automobiles were the main source of photochemical smog.

Public officials and representatives of citizens' groups in California complained to their state and national legislators. Hearings were held at the state capital and in Washington, D.C. The National Academy of Sciences in Washington was asked to form a panel to review the scientific and technical aspects of the problem. During the 1960s and early 1970s, the National Research Council (part of the National Academy) produced a series of increasingly negative reports.

Some form of regulation was obviously needed. However, government officials—particularly, those in the newly established Environmental Protection Agency (EPA)—were unsure of a solution to the problem. They considered restricting the use of automobiles to certain days of the week. (That method is now employed in Athens, Greece, where the climate and other factors are similar to those in Los Angeles. It has not been very successful.)

After much thought, legislators in Congress and officials at the EPA sought a technical solution to the problem. They reasoned that smog would be greatly reduced if pollution could be stopped at the source. The experts determined to find a way to reduce or eliminate the pollutants found in automobile exhaust fumes. These pollutants include gaseous oxides of nitrogen and other impurities. Automobile exhaust also contains carbon monoxide (CO), which is toxic by itself. A car going one mile (about 1.6 kilometers) generates almost one ounce of carbon monoxide (28 grams). To dilute this toxic gas to a safe level requires about 2 million quarts of air (1.9 million liters). In other words, the dilution factor is 64,000,000 to 1.

For 20 years, scientists and engineers affiliated with universities and private industry worked on the problem of removing contaminants from auto exhausts. Progress was slow because little basic research had been done before the crisis. In fact, most previous research on the chemistry of nitrogen was

Smog in the Los Angeles basin. Photo taken around the mid-1950s.
(Courtesy of the Environmental Protection Agency)

directed toward development of nitrogenous fertilizers. That procedure included the capture of pure nitrogen gas and transforming it into nitrogen oxides. Such chemical reactions had exactly the opposite effect compared to reducing nitrogen oxides to pure nitrogen, which is not a pollutant.

Finally, the scientists and engineers provided a solution to the problem of smog control. They designed a device known as a catalytic converter. The converter is a small canister connected to the exhaust pipe of a vehicle. It contains a series of ceramic screens coated with platinum and other rare metals. Chemicals in the hot gases generated by a gasoline engine pass through the canister and are broken down into relatively harmless molecules. In a complicated sequence, each metal acts upon a different pollutant. Nitrogen oxide becomes molecules of pure oxygen and pure nitrogen. Unburned gasoline, carbon monoxide, and particles of carbon-based substances are broken down into water vapor and carbon dioxide. The carbon dioxide gas is the only contaminant that remains. The problem of California's smog had been moderated.

For a few years, people who lived in other areas of the United States had been rather indifferent to the smog in Los Angeles. They considered themselves better situated than the poor smog-plagued Angelenos. However, it soon became apparent that many other cities—some of modest size—were also susceptible to the problem.

By 1975, photochemical smog was beginning to appear in many cities. That same year, officials of the Environmental Protection Agency (EPA) put forth a regulation to improve the situation. They decreed that the newly designed catalytic converter must be installed in most cars manufactured in 1976. The following year, the requirement applied to every new automobile and truck manufactured in the United States.

The timing was not good for several reasons. The converters were still rather crude and not fully efficient. Also, citizens of the United States were experiencing a serious gasoline short-

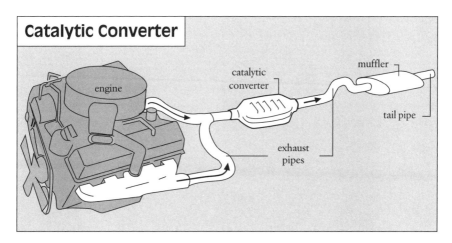

Catalytic Converter

A catalytic converter is installed in a car's exhaust system in front of the muffler. It converts exhaust gases to pure nitrogen, water and carbon dioxide.

age. A petroleum embargo had resulted from political developments in the Near East, and little oil was reaching refineries in the United States. People were concerned about trying any new device that might increase the need for gasoline.

In addition to the other problems, many groups in the United States were opposed to the required installation of catalytic converters. Auto manufacturers saw the addition of this device as interfering with attempts to hold down their costs. Some people claimed that the catalytic converters reduced the efficiency of the car's engine and increased fuel consumption. These claims were generally untrue but widely believed. Many new car buyers broke the law by paying a mechanic to remove the device. The owners believed that they were conserving precious gasoline by their illegal act.

In their haste to solve a dangerous problem, regulators had mandated the use of catalytic converters before they were fully perfected. Converters installed in the first few years of the EPA ruling were worn out before the car became outmoded. It was not until 1980 that the catalytic action could continue to perform for 50,000 miles (80,000 km). Today, the technical standard of converter performance requires at least 100,000 miles (160,000 km) of service.

ENFORCEMENT

The functioning of catalytic converters can be monitored by regular inspections. Since the early 1980s, 28 states and the District of Columbia have required periodic testing for automobiles registered in high-traffic areas. The exhaust gases are sampled, and the amount of contaminants is determined. If the car does not pass the test, the converter must be replaced at the owner's expense.

Fuel Complications

In 1921, a chemist, Thomas Midgley, Jr., discovered that the addition of lead allowed the gasoline used in automobile engines to burn more evenly. Carbon-based molecules containing lead were first introduced as gasoline additives in the mid-1920s. Although the lead added to the engine's efficiency, it later proved to be one of the contaminating materials in automobile exhausts.

In the late 1940s, medical research indicated that lead ingested in food and drinking water was a danger to health. Lead—found in particles of old paint and other substances—caused retardation in children, problems of the central nervous system, and impairment of kidney function. In the 1950s and 1960s, public health officials began a campaign to reduce the amount of lead taken into the human body.

As the number of automobiles increased, lead from their exhaust was also found to be a significant source of lead poisoning. In addition, scientists discovered that the lead that affected human well-being destroyed the catalytic action of converters. Therefore, the legally mandated use of converters brought an end to the use of leaded gasoline. Petroleum companies were forced to provide lead-free gasoline to preserve the usefulness of catalytic converters. Thus, the introduction of catalytic converters has had two beneficial results. Lead-free gasoline eliminates lead emissions, and catalytic action greatly reduces the amount of smog-producing gas. Other nonmetallic chemicals are now used to perform the same functions as lead in gasoline.

Catalytic converters operate at a very high temperature. The device remains hot for several minutes after a car is parked and the motor is turned off. Unfortunately, in those few minutes, the hot converter—located on the underside of the car—could start a fire in a pile of leaves, for instance. In 1996, engineers at the National Renewable Energy Laboratory and at Benteler Industries, Inc. have developed a special insulating cap that fits over the catalytic converter. The cap shields the surrounding area from the intense heat generated by the converter. It also retains the heat so that when the driver restarts the engine after a brief interval, the still-hot converter is ready to perform. Because the catalytic converter must be hot to remove pollutants, the insulating cap helps improve the converter's performance while preventing accidental fires.

Smog Remains

Unfortunately, the smog problem is still not totally eliminated. The catalytic converter can remove only 90 percent of the harmful emissions. Also, the number of automobiles on the highways of the United States continues to grow. Consequently, after a temporary decline, the amount of nitrogen oxides and unburned fuel particles is increasing again. Several conditions contribute to this resurgence. Engineers have succeeded in designing cars that last longer. Even in the newest models, car engines and catalytic systems become less efficient over time. In general, cars more than 10 years old are the biggest offenders. Some environmental research organizations estimate that 10 percent of the automobiles generate more than 50 percent of the pollution. That 10 percent includes most of the older cars.

California and other states have considered a program of buying older cars from their owners. However, forcing citizens to sell their older cars is not politically sound. Many citizens believe that this policy would be unwarranted government interference in their lives.

Additional technical solutions are on the horizon. After early enthusiasm and many later disappointments, progress is being made to fabricate a car that runs on electricity. Since electric power generation also produces some pollution, the electric car is not a perfect answer. If car engines are redesigned, the use of alternate fuels such as natural gas (methane) could improve the situation. Natural gas produces much less pollution-causing nitrogen oxides than other fuels. However, with today's technologies, neither electricity nor natural gas would offer a complete solution to the problem.

One of the most appealing alternative fuels is pure hydrogen. It is very efficient and generates only water vapor as an emission. However, pure hydrogen can be costly to produce and its use will require changes in engine design.

Nontechnical Adaptations

For several decades, people have tried various programs to reduce automobile use. Car pooling is one such program. Many states, notably Virginia, have reserved express lanes on major highways for vehicles that carry more than one person. This practice provides an incentive to car pool because driving on the uncongested express lanes is faster and less stressful. As an added benefit, each member of the car pool saves money on gasoline and car repairs. Also, many people like the companionship.

Other programs sponsored by local or regional governments include the expansion or restoration of mass transit systems such as buses and subways. In relatively recent times, subways have been built in the metropolitan areas of San Francisco, California, and Washington, D.C. Modern subways are an excellent solution to traffic and pollution problems. The amount of pollution produced per passenger trip is far lower than that generated by an automobile.

In Europe and Asia, the bicycle has long been an important mode of transportation. Urban planners in the United States have tried various methods—such as specially marked bike lanes—to popularize bicycling in the United States. However, except for purely recreational purposes, the use of bicycles for transportation has been limited mainly to young people.

In spite of some success in the programs to reduce photochemical smog, this type of pollution remains a major problem.

7
Acid Rain

For many years, emissions from smelting and other industrial facilities have caused damage to nearby property. Fortunately, restrictions on industrial practices have partially solved the problem. However, the danger of pollution remains.

The combustion, or burning, of fossil fuels—coal and oil—releases gases that can generate acid rain. This threat occurs when the gases of sulfur dioxide (SO_2) and nitrogen oxides combine with oxygen and moisture in the atmosphere. The molecules of nitrogen oxides then form nitric acid (HNO_3) and the molecules of sulfur dioxide form sulfuric acid (H_2SO_4). To complete the process, the acid is dissolved in drops of rain and eventually falls to the ground. Forests, fields, gardens, and aquatic plants are harmed by these chemicals.

Sulfur emissions are the most important cause of acid rain. In the United States, electric utility companies produce 70 percent of the airborne sulfur dioxide. In 1980, the smokestacks of electric power plants in the United States sent 11 million tons of sulfur dioxide into the Earth's atmosphere.

Nitrogen oxide—the other chemical responsible for acid rain—results from the combustion of oil, gasoline, and jet fuel. Although both chemicals are harmful, scientists have found that the acid rain attributable to nitrogen oxide tends to be more local than that caused by sulfurous gases.

A major difference between the effects of sulfurous smog and acid rain is the size of the affected area. The aftermath of

Smokestack emissions from a metal-smelting plant in New Orleans
(Courtesy of the Environmental Protection Agency)

smog is a local problem, while acid rain damage can extend over a very large area. Moreover, the areas damaged by acid rain can be found hundreds of miles from the source of pollution. The contaminated smoke is sent high into the air by the heat of combustion and the height of the smokestacks. Strong winds can carry the damaging gases for long distances before they fall to the ground.

In North America, the chemicals that form aid rain are carried from west to east by the prevailing winds. Wind-blown sulfurous smoke from electric power companies in midwestern states travels hundreds of miles before descending as acid rain in the northeast. Areas along much of the Atlantic seacoast have been harmed by this pollution. Officials of Canada's eastern provinces and the New England states have reason to be upset by the emissions from these power plants.

Although acid rain poses no direct health hazard to humans, it attacks paint on buildings and erodes limestone structures and sculptures. It reduces food crop production and can kill or dwarf pine trees. In higher, more exposed locations, spruce trees and fir trees in New York, Vermont, and New Hampshire have been destroyed. Acid rain has weakened trees in the forests of Tennessee, Virginia, and North Carolina. The damaged trees become vulnerable to insects and soon die.

Acid rain can sterilize lakes by increasing the acid content of lake water. The acid kills the small plants that feed the small

When acid rain falls on the leaves of growing trees, normal photosynthesis is impaired. Some trees will die if the stress is prolonged. Some evergreens in this stand of trees in Europe have died because of acid rain.
(Courtesy of Dr. Guenther Eichhorn)

Acid rain attacks many materials. Limestone, a common material used by masons and sculptors, is particularly vulnerable. At one time, this limestone tomb was capped by a fine sculpture, but the stone has now eroded to a ruin. (Courtesy of Alexander Murashov, East Carolina University)

fish that are eaten by large fish. Sport fishing is an important part of the tourist industry in Canada and the northeastern United States. When lakes become barren, the tourist business declines.

In the early 1980s, the problem of acid rain strained relations between Canada and the United States. Canadian political officials wanted the United States to regulate sulfur dioxide emissions or pay compensation to Canadian enterprises—or both. The discussions became heated, but no solution was forthcoming. Negotiators for the U.S. government saw that restraints on electric power generation would have negative political and economic consequences in the midwestern states. However, when states all along the east coast began to complain about the situation, the U.S. government finally was forced to take action. At first, utility companies were encouraged to reduce emissions on a voluntary basis. Then new, stronger regulations were added to existing laws. In 1983, the Federal Air Quality Act was passed, and in 1990 it was revised to further the control of emissions.

Under the provisions of this act, regulators were required to study the records of each utility company. From this information, they calculated the amount of sulfur dioxide that had been generated by each factory in the preceding years. Because sulfur dioxide gas is the most frequent pollutant, this figure determines the tonnage of pollutants, or allowances, allotted to each factory or power plant.

Each allowance is equal to one ton of sulfur dioxide emissions. If a company had a history of putting 3,000 tons of sulfur dioxide into the air every year, it was allotted 3,000 allowances. No more allowances would be issued even if the utility company expanded its power production level. Therefore, under the new plan, the company could produce 3,000 tons of pollutants without penalty. If it generated less than its allotted amount, it could sell the extra allowances to another company. On the other hand, if the company generated more sulfur dioxide than allowed, it is required to buy additional allowances from some other utility company. If it does not, the government applies a penalty of $2,000 per ton of unallotted pollutants.

The purpose of the Federal Air Quality Act of 1990 was to prevent an increase in pollution at the same time that the demand for electricity expanded. However, officials hoped that the effects of the law would gradually decrease the level of pollution. To the surprise of many environmentalists, this scheme has worked reasonably well. The rate of sulfur dioxide emission in 1980 was about 17.3 million tons per year. By 1995, the emission level had been reduced to a bit more than 11.9 million tons. By 2001, the amount was 10.8 million tons—so while the reduction is slowing, it is still substantial.

While many New Englanders and Canadians are still dissatisfied, the Environmental Protection Agency is pleased with the record. They point to the increasing demand for electricity between 1980 and 1995. In earlier years, this increase would have resulted in a higher pollution level. The Air Quality Act has brought about a cleaner environment at the same time that most utilities companies enjoyed high employment and economic prosperity.

Technical Responses

The new rules and regulations caused the managers of utility companies to investigate ways of reducing pollution from their power plants. Scientists sought methods to decrease the amount of contamination caused by coal smoke. Therefore, they set out to remove some of the sulfur products that are present in coal.

Two types of coal are mined in the United States. Anthracite, or hard, coal has a high carbon content, a low sulfur content, few impurities, and burns with a clean flame. Bituminous, or soft, coal contains many complicated carbon compounds, more sulfur, many impurities, and burns with a smoky flame that generates many pollutants. The hard coals are therefore superior to the soft coals for pollution control. However, the hard coals are more expensive. Consequently, special techniques for "washing" bituminous coal have been developed.

When soft coal is mined, relatively small quantities of the surrounding rock, sand, and gravel are extracted with the ore. All of these materials contain unwanted sulfur compounds and various other impurities. In order to separate the coal from the unwanted materials, the newly mined coal is dumped on conveyor belts, and strong jets of water or air are directed at the mixture of coal and rock. Because coal is lighter than rock, the force of the water or air moves the pieces of coal away from the heavier rock. Although the washing process does not change the sulfur content of the coal, it physically separates the coal from the mix of heavier, sulfur-rich rock and gravel. These foreign materials are discarded, and the coal is made ready for shipping.

Although washing coal reduces the amount of pollutants, this technique does not eliminate the pollution problem. To help correct the situation, engineers designed a new type of furnace that allows more efficient combustion of coal and better air circulation. These advanced furnaces, often used to generate electricity, have special fire grates called fluidized beds. The grate—or fire bed—is composed of a solid piece of sheet metal. Air pipes perforated with holes are attached to the top of the sheet and blanketed with sand or finely ground limestone. Coal is laid on the top and set afire. Air blown through the pipes escapes through the holes and travels upward through the sand or limestone. The air supports the burning process. The sand, constantly shifted by the force of the air currents, distributes the heat evenly over the fire bed. If limestone is used under the burning coal (in a fluidized limestone furnace), some of the sulfur released by combustion is absorbed immediately by the limestone ($CaCO_2$) to make non-polluting calcium sulfate ($CaSO_4$). However, a covering of sand (as used in a fluidized sand furnace) might be a better choice for many industries. This type of furnace can use a wide range of fuels. Coal, solid waste, or trash—even wet garbage—can be burned in such furnaces.

Smokestack technology has also improved. Both soot and sulfur dioxide are reduced when smoke is passed through a scrubber. Several forms of smoke scrubbers are in use. In one version, a set of metal screens directs the smoke to an adjacent horizontal chamber. Here, the smoke is sprayed with water or with a water solution of neutralizing chemicals. In other systems, the smoke is directed into the bottom of a nearby tank and bubbled up through a cleansing solution. As the smoke passes through the solution, many pollutants are collected in the liquid. When it can absorb no more pollutants, the solution is drained into a pool, and the solids settle to the bottom. The water—which contains the dissolved chemicals—then flows through an electrically charged screen. The electric charge attracts the molecules of carbon compounds and sulfur dioxide that resulted from the combustion of fossil fuels. The now-purified liquid is recycled. Chemicals collected from the pools and the screens are sold to other industries.

These new techniques can transform former industrial waste into valuable products. Sulfur dioxide gas can be collected and transformed immediately into sulfuric acid. This acid is used in industrial processes such as the manufacture of dyes and paints. Where oil is used as a fuel, ammonia is retrieved by stack scrubbers and provides the raw material to produce fertilizers.

Engineering technology is not the only advanced method of pollution control. Researchers in Europe and elsewhere are focusing on other approaches to the problem of acid rain. For example, Scandinavian scientists are looking for new ways to control the effects of acid rain after it has fallen. In these countries, damage results when winds carry pollutants from the highly industrialized areas to the east and south of Scandinavia. The acid rain falls into Scandinavian lakes and destroys the aquatic plants that feed the fish. Scientists are attempting to reduce the acid concentration in lake water by adding pulverized limestone. They believe that the limestone will neutralize the acids and make the water more hospitable to life.

Remaining Issues

While the trading of pollution permits has reduced pollution from the smokestacks of the electric power plants, there is still much to be done before the air in southeastern Canada and the northeastern United States is truly clean. The underlying facts were brought out by a team of alert meteorologists from the University of Maryland. Starting in the late 1990s, team members periodically sampled pollution levels in the northeastern states. They had made extensive measurements in the summer of 2002. In August 2003, parts of Canada, Ohio, Pennsylvania, New York, and most of New England experienced a catastrophic failure of the high-voltage system that supplies the region with electricity. Consequently, almost all the power plants in the region were forced to shut down so that distribution transformers and other equipment would not suffer from acute overloads. The result was a regionwide blackout with negative effects on regional industries, families and individuals. However, there was one bright side.

The day following the blackout, the Maryland team was airborne and was sampling pollutants in their base area, the Washington–New York corridor. They saw the unique opportunity to measure the air downwind of major power plants that were idle and compare their readings with those made almost exactly a year before when the plants were active.

The results revealed a 90 percent drop in sulfur oxides that cause acid rain, a 50 percent drop in the nitrogen oxides that generate smog, and an increase of aerial visibility of 40 miles (64 km). These figures go far in defining the work that remains to be done to achieve clean air.

Toxic Substances

8

In the tradition of environmentalists, toxic industrial chemicals have not been considered prominently as air pollutants. However, recent events and public concern about the threats from terrorism have made both industrial chemicals and poison gas a central topic. Some history is needed to put these issues in perspective.

For example, both the Allied forces (England, France, and Italy) and the Central powers (Germany, Austria, and Turkey) used poison gases in World War I. The German army first used chlorine gas dispensed from steel containers against the French army in 1915. These actions were only partly effective because of shifts in the wind direction. Poisonous mustard gas was incorporated into artillery shells in 1917, and both sides used these with more effective outcomes by 1917. The net effect of poison gas use was a death toll of more than 25,000 by the French, British, and German armies by the war's end in 1918.

In the 1930s, the Italian army under Mussolini used gas attacks against the Ethiopian army. However, few civilians were at risk until 1988, when Iraqi dictator Saddam Hussein ordered his forces to use a mixture of different types of gas bombs against the Kurdish people of northern Iraq. Before these attacks, such incidents were considered odd, ill advised, and aberrant because the use of gas has serious military drawbacks.

The effectiveness of a gas attack depends on atmospheric conditions that are totally uncontrollable and only partially predictable. Consequently, the victims of such assaults might be friendly to the attackers. An unexpected change in wind direction could easily cause the gas to drift into the wrong area.

On the strategic level, the main problem is that everyone, not just combatants, is harmed by contact with poison gas. Civilians—including innocent women and children—are as likely to become victims as are those for whom the gas is intended. Because of this consequence, most nations, including the United States, have signed international agreements to outlaw the use of poison gas. Governments that ignore such agreements can be punished by political and economic sanctions. However, the very properties that make poison gas unattractive to responsible government officials and military commanders make it attractive to terrorists.

Now, in 2005, terrorism has become a central concern for top government officials. In the United States, a new cabinet-level organization of government, the Department of Homeland Security, has been established to prevent or aid recovery from a poison gas attack by terrorists.

Industrial Chemicals

In 2003, elected representatives of both major political parties offered new legislation to reduce the vulnerability of chemical storage facilities in the United States. Officials in the Environmental Protection Agency (EPA) identified almost 3,000 sites where a chemical release could cause at least 10,000 or more casualties. Among the 3,000 sites are 123 chemical plants that, if successfully sabotaged by terrorists, could produce as many as 1 million casualties. Such estimates might seem excessive but at least one chemical storage incident resulted in several thousand, immediate deaths. Such a disaster took place at a chemical plant in Bhopal, India. Around midnight on December 3, 1984, tons of methyl isocyanate, which is used to make pesticides, rapidly leaked from a storage tank. The plant was partially owned and operated by Union Carbide of India, Ltd. A parent company, Union Carbide, Inc., of the United States, owned 51 percent of the stock. The Indian government owned a large block of stock, and mainly Indian private citizens owned the remainder. This arrangement has made legal actions on the part of the victims very difficult.

Figures from different sources vary, but it seems clear that the gas killed well over 3,000 people immediately and that thousands more died in the days and weeks that followed. Many others were disabled, and there are claims that lingering illnesses, caused by the chemical, affect the local residents even to the present time.

When a disaster of such magnitude strikes, strong emotions are released. Guilt and denial tend to be prominent. In the face of such reactions, it is not surprising that the actual cause of the incident remains uncertain. The owners and managers have one view. The victims and their families have another. In any case, the owners—under court order—have paid some of the victims' compensation claims. Disputes continue, however, over the responsibility for cleaning the site of toxic residues. Neither the owners nor the Indian government will accept the cost and responsibility for the cleanup.

At the present time, the main problem for scientists and public officials is that large storage tanks of hazardous chemicals are analogous to poison gas weapons. The deadly chemicals can be released either by accident or by sabotage. Little has been done by the owners or by government agencies to upgrade security at chemical storage sites.

Storage tanks for chemical and petroleum products near Long Beach, California (Courtesy of Wilton S. Taft, photographer)

Harm Reduction

The actions to be taken to prevent a chemical release or to limit the bad effects are primarily in the realm of management rather than science. For example, the owners of facilities where toxic or dangerous chemicals are stored in large quantities could strengthen site security by putting up fences and using armed guards. High costs have apparently limited the extent of such changes.

Fortunately, provisions to control the bad effects of an accidental release are much the same as the provisions needed to limit the effects of sabotage. For the owners and operators of a vulnerable chemical factory or tank farm, the goal is containment. If the threat comes from a chemical in liquid form, earthen dykes are a possible response. Otherwise, digging channels so that the dangerous liquid will run into holding pits is an option. However, if the substance is a gas or can form an airborne mist, these actions will not be of much help. Emergency and security personnel who are employed by the owners can be key agents in such situations by simply reducing or cutting-off the flow of dangerous materials.

For local government officials, a possible response is evacuation. A successful evacuation will depend on prompt warning from the disaster site and the presence of a transportation plan that minimizes congestion and confusion. Government officials are also usually responsible for providing the emergency backup personnel in the form of police, fire fighters, and paramedics—collectively known as first responders. Events such as the Twin Towers disaster in New York City have provided lessons in likely areas of breakdown. For example, if the first responders have different and conflicting lines of command authority, coordinated actions can be difficult. Specifically, communications equipment must be compatible between the emergency services and the rules-of-use of common channels must be clear and easily followed.

The transportation of hazardous materials offers some special problems. For example, much of the freight that comes into the United States from foreign sources is carried in special containers that can be carried aboard ships and readily converted to truck or rail conveyance. Such containers remain unopened from point of departure to destination and could hold dangerous materials without that fact being known to the transporters.

Also, many bulk chemicals are transported by rail in tank cars. Officials of the Department of Homeland Security and the Environmental Protection Agency have suggested that tank cars carrying compounds that could react with one another should not be carried in adjacent positions in the train. The carriers have not adopted this practice because the makeup of trains has traditionally been determined by other factors, such as the destination of each freight car.

Where Science Enters

There are two main ways in which scientists can contribute to an improvement in chemical security. One is related to the use of chemical raw materials in manufacturing processes. The goal is the adoption of benign or harmless chemicals in place of those that are toxic or dangerous. A good example of such a substitution is the use of a material called supercritical carbon dioxide as a solvent and as a carrier of reagents in chemical synthesis reactions. Many of the most commonly used organic solvents, such as ether, benzene, or acetone, are either toxic or highly inflammable or both. The most common inorganic solvent is water, but the problem with the use of water is that once used, the water is contaminated and must be decontaminated before it is discharged as wastewater. Supercritical carbon dioxide is not toxic in any way and is used in a closed system so that the solvent is never released into the atmosphere or waterways.

Also, there is an environmental benefit because the carbon dioxide can be drawn from sources such as the chimneys of power plants that are burning a fossil fuel which would otherwise be adding to the greenhouse effect.

Carbon dioxide exists naturally as a gas. However, it can be compressed and frozen into a solid—known commonly as dry ice. Carbon dioxide does not form a liquid phase in its natural state. When the dry ice "melts," it goes directly from the solid phase to the gas phase. The gas can be made to act like a liquid only if it is put under very high pressure. When put into such a liquid state, its condition is called supercritical, and its power as a solvent comes to the fore.

Carbon dioxide in this liquid form will dissolve many chemicals at room temperature. Important chemical reactions can take place between two chemicals when both are dissolved in supercritical carbon dioxide.

One famous use of supercritical carbon dioxide is in the decaffeination of coffee. Coffee is placed in the reaction chamber and supercritical carbon dioxide is piped in. The carbon dioxide in its liquid phase is very penetrating. If the temperature is just right, it will dissolve the caffeine but leave the flavorful agents behind. When the liquid is pumped into another chamber, the temperature can be changed. Then, the caffeine comes out of solution and is deposited in this second chamber, and the supercritical carbon dioxide can be recycled.

The second way that science can support increased protection from chemical disasters is through the development of better detectors. If specialized detectors were deployed on the grounds of a chemical plant, they could be tuned to detect small quantities of the particular toxic material that was being used in the manufacturing process. Such detectors could be attached to an alarm system so that if a leak occurred, early warning would be assured.

Good progress is being made in the development of small, rugged, and sensitive detectors. So far, most have narrow applications. For example, sensors have been planted underground near buried gasoline storage tanks. If a leak occurs, it is detected early and actions can be taken to stop the leak before the toxic material enters the water supply.

Other similar devices have been developed for use at airport checkpoints. These "sniffers" are tuned to detect the gases that are given off in tiny amounts by various explosive materials. The detectors are used to inspect luggage so that no one can carry an explosive package aboard an aircraft.

The most modern portable sensors use an array of sensitive crystals on the intake side so that patterns of signals can be used to analyze the exact composition of a mixture of chemi-

Lightweight, rugged detectors or chemical "sniffers" are needed to moni-
tor possible leaks or breakdowns of containment of toxic materials.
Department of Energy technicians are testing models of such devices.
(Courtesy of the Department of Energy)

cals. The analysis is done by a miniature computer that is integrated into the sensor package so that the sensor is easily
portable and readings can be made almost instantaneously.
Work is proceeding to make such devices more sensitive without increasing the rate of false alarms.

9

Ozone Depletion

Ozone is a strange substance. Depending on the altitude, it can be life-giving or deadly. When ozone is present at or near the surface of the earth, it is toxic to plants and animals. At that level, ozone is corrosive and acts much like an acid. It causes eye irritation, raw throats, and lung inflammation. For those with asthma or other respiratory diseases, ozone can be fatal. High concentrations of ozone are found in photochemical smog. This type of urban pollution results from a mix of automobile exhaust fumes, bright sunlight, and stagnant air. In 1996, research workers from the Harvard School of Public Health estimated that photochemical smog in the United States is responsible for more than 50,000 hospital cases a year.

In sharp contrast, ozone in the stratosphere—the atmosphere above 30,000 feet (9,000 m)—is vital to the well-being of every plant and animal on the surface of the Earth. The ozone in the upper atmosphere shields the planet from invisible but harmful ultraviolet rays of the Sun. If such rays hit the Earth full force, they would kill fish and shrimp larvae near the surface of the oceans, stunt the growth of plants, and contribute to vision problems and skin cancer in humans.

The chemical nature of ozone was discovered in 1840 by a German chemist, Christian Schonbein. He found that ozone is a molecule composed of three oxygen atoms (O_3). At the time, electrical discharges were thought to transform ordinary oxygen (O_2) into ozone. Both natural discharges such as lightning or artificial discharges such as sparks made by electrical laboratory equipment were regarded as possible causes. Schonbein found that an ozone molecule was rather fragile because it soon reverted spontaneously to a molecule of ordinary oxygen.

In 1881, a British chemistry teacher, W. N. Hartley, very carefully experimented with ozone. He found that ozone in the atmosphere absorbs a certain portion of the Sun's radiation. Charles Fabry, a French physicist, confirmed Hartley's findings in 1913. With the use of high-altitude balloons, Fabry established that ozone was concentrated in the stratosphere at a height of about 60,000 feet (18,000 m). In subsequent research, chemists and physiologists found that the filtering action of ozone was beneficial to life on Earth. They concluded that advanced life-forms could not have developed if the harmful portion of the Sun's radiation had not been blocked. In other words, the ozone shield is essential to life on this planet.

Early Warning

In the late 1960s, the political movement to protect the environment was beginning to gather strength. Many people were afraid that their home planet was being spoiled. The overuse of insecticides such as DDT was debated in congressional hearings and in the law courts. Public concern was aroused by the growing problems of urban smog and acid rain.

Scientific advisers to the U.S. government encouraged the National Science Foundation (NSF) to sponsor a broad international survey on the condition of the atmosphere. Officials of the NSF recruited Carroll L. Wilson and W. H. Matthews. The two men were prominent members of the faculty at the Massachusetts Institute of Technology. In turn, Wilson and Matthews gathered a team of scientists to report on the status of environmental research and the contents of scientific literature on the subject. The Ford Foundation, the American

Conservation Association, and the Alfred P. Sloan Foundation provided additional funding for this project. A report, published in early 1971, covered a wide range of environmental problems ranging from photochemical smog to the disposal of solid wastes such as household garbage.

Later in 1971, staff members of the United Nations (UN) held an international conference in Oslo, Norway, to review the state of the worldwide environment. Organizers included personnel from the World Meteorological Organization and the International Council of Scientific Unions—both affiliated with the United Nations. The reports edited by Matthews and Wilson provided the conference members with material for their discussions.

In late 1971, shortly after the UN meetings, NASA scientists declared that exhaust products from the proposed space shuttle might injure the ozone layer. At the time, various rocket engines were being tested by NASA engineers. They determined that all of the engines generated exhaust products that contained oxides of nitrogen and small amounts of chlorine compounds. For the first time, the stratosphere might be polluted by potentially dangerous, man-made chemicals.

The year before, a Dutch chemist and meteorologist, Paul Crutzen, (now working at the Max Planck Institute for Chemistry), had established that nitrogen oxides could attack ozone. He also discovered that a single molecule of nitric oxide in the stratosphere could set up a chain reaction and destroy many molecules of ozone. The concerns of the space scientists were given some coverage in newspapers and newsmagazines. However, the general public was not interested. The shuttle program was still far in the future.

Another possible environmental problem involved the flight of supersonic transport aircraft (SST). In the early 1970s, this type of aircraft was in the initial stages of development by manufacturers in the United States, England, France, and the Soviet Union. Advocates imagined a fleet of thousands of these aircraft carrying passengers and freight at high speed on long-distance flights. However, environmentalists saw the negative side of an SST fleet. From the publicity surrounding the space shuttle problems, they learned that exhaust fumes from the SST jet engines would generate large amounts of nitrogen oxides. These were the chemicals that Crutzen had shown to attack and destroy ozone. The SSTs would reach the stratosphere, bringing injurious exhaust products near the ozone shield. This time the public was roused to action. Conservationist groups such as the Sierra Club and the World Wildlife Federation sent protests to the U.S. Congress.

Officials of the National Aeronautics and Space Administration, the Department of Defense, and other government bodies finally decided that the SST was not a sound investment. They were not so much impressed by the possible damage to the ozone layer as they were by revelations that the SST would never make a profit. The Soviets had pursued the development of an SST, but abandoned their efforts after their first aircraft crashed at an international airshow. However, a team of British and French engineers designed the Concorde, an SST that flies beautifully. Several such aircraft were built by a combination of French and British companies. As predicted, however, the Concorde was economically unsound and lost money for 20 years. Therefore, few SSTs were built, and they were retired from service in 2003.

The ozone layer was further protected when NASA engineers modified the composition of the shuttle fuel to minimize the release of oxides of nitrogen. Without a threat from the space shuttle or the SST, the future seemed safe for the ozone layer. Nevertheless, scientists continued to investigate various aspects of the upper atmosphere. In 1970, James Lovelock, an English scientist, was investigating high-level air currents. While studying large air masses such as the jet stream, he encountered the chemical trichloro-monofluoro-methane. For convenience, this family of chemicals is known as chlorofluorocarbons, or CFCs.

The molecule consists of one central carbon atom linked to two, or sometimes three, chlorine atoms.

James Lovelock was not alarmed by the discovery of CFCs in the stratosphere. He had been assured by fellow scientists that this chemical was extremely stable. CFCs had been invented in 1930 by Thomas Midgley, Jr., the same man who developed leaded gasoline. While employed by the General Motors Corporation, the chemist had been searching for a gas to use in automobile air conditioners. The gas needed to be highly stable, nontoxic, and compressible. Midgely knew that

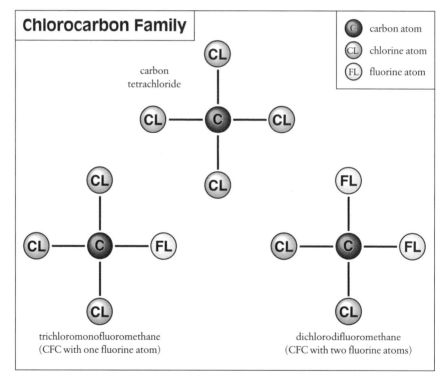

The chlorocarbon family has three principal members: carbon tetrachloride and two chlorofluorocarbon (CFC) molecules—trichloromonofluoromethane and dichlorodifluoromethane.

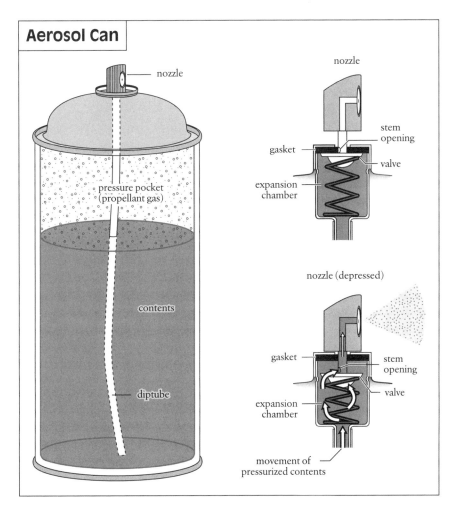

Aerosol Can

nozzle

nozzle

stem opening

gasket

valve

expansion chamber

pressure pocket (propellant gas)

contents

diptube

nozzle (depressed)

gasket

stem opening

valve

expansion chamber

movement of pressurized contents

Pressing the button on the top of this aerosol can releases the vaporized contents as a spray. Such cans are still in use but no longer use CFCs as the propellant gas.

carbon tetrachloride was a common, highly stable liquid with four chlorine atoms attached to one carbon atom (CCl_4). He reasoned that by substituting a lighter element, fluorine (F), for some of the heavier chlorine in the carbon tetrachloride molecule, he could make a stable gas. He was correct. Thus, the gaseous CFCs were born.

At first, CFCs were used almost exclusively in air-conditioning and refrigeration systems. Soon, the gases were found useful for cleaning oil or grease from delicate metal parts. Food processors tried CFCs for flash-freezing foods. The idea worked well because CFCs were nontoxic and did not react with the foods or any other chemicals.

In the late 1940s, Robert H. Abplanalp invented a device called an aerosol dispenser. The dispenser could be installed in a canister containing a propellant gas. At the touch of a button, the propellant forced a portion of any liquid inside the canister to escape through a small nozzle. Depending on the desired consistency, the liquid was dispensed in the form of a strong spray such as hair spray, or as a foam such as shaving cream. The dispenser device could be mass-produced so that each one cost a very small amount of money. The invention became immediately popular. Deodorants, paints, insecticides, whipped cream—indeed, anything that could be sprayed— was soon being dispensed by Abplanalp's device. In 1973, almost 3 billion aerosol containers were sold in the United States. The propellant gases were CFCs, which were ideal for the purpose.

The Ozone Killer

In 1971, F. Sherwood Rowland, a chemist at the University of California at Irvine, became curious about Lovelock's discovery of CFCs in the stratosphere. Because CFCs are relatively heavy gases, Rowland was surprised that they have been found so high in the atmosphere. Although they were known as stable gases, he wondered whether the CFCs in the upper atmosphere would break down under the full impact of the Sun's energy. Rowland's area of specialization was the chemistry of irradiated atoms, and he became interested in the long-term stability of CFCs.

Rowland was born in 1928 in Delaware, Ohio. He remained in Delaware to attend Ohio Wesleyan University, where he played varsity baseball and basketball. His graduate work was done at the University of Chicago. There he studied under Willard F. Libby, who won a Nobel Prize for his work on radioactivity.

After receiving his Ph.D., Rowland was awarded a four-year research appointment at Princeton University. He then taught at the University of Kansas. He was only 36 years old when he was invited to become the chair of the new department of chemistry at the University of California at Irvine (UCI).

Rowland had established a reputation for being a careful, unbiased research scientist who was interested in environmental issues. Early in his career at UCI, California officials asked him to determine the degree of mercury contamination in tuna caught off their coast. Environmentalists were convinced that the level of industrial contamination was high. They believed that consumers were being exposed to mercuric poisoning by eating the California tuna. After a careful study of the fish, Rowland determined that they contained no more mercury than fish caught in the 1940s.

In 1972, Rowland invited Mario Molina, a Mexican scientist, to join an investigation of CFCs. Molina had recently completed his Ph.D.

F. Sherwood Rowland discovered that chlorine was released by the CFC molecules that reached the stratosphere. (Courtesy of the University of California at Irvine)

Mario Molina was Rowland's partner in the research on CFCs.
(Courtesy of the University of California at Irvine)

in atmospheric chemistry at the University of California at Berkeley. The two researchers planned the study together.

Meanwhile, another project was under way at the University of Michigan in Ann Arbor. Research engineers Richard Stolarski and Ralph Cicerone were still intrigued by the possibility that the exhaust from the space shuttles might damage the ozone layer. Because other chemists were already studying the effects of nitrogen oxides on ozone, Stolarski and Cicerone decided to investigate the effects of free chlorine. This choice seemed logical because, at that time, small but detectable amounts of chlorine compounds were found in emissions from solid rocket fuel. The officials at the National Aeronautics and Space Administration (NASA) agreed to provide funding for their study.

Stolarski and Cicerone found that free chlorine actively destroys ozone. Furthermore, after a chlorine atom attacks and destroys a molecule of ozone, the same atom of chlorine remains free to destroy other ozone molecules. In short, a small amount of chlorine can destroy a large amount of ozone.

In 1973, the results of this research were presented at a NASA-sponsored meeting in Kyoto, Japan. This report and many others were summarized in a special edition of the *Canadian Journal of Chemistry*. The findings of Stolarski and Cicerone were confirmed by a similar study reported by Michael McElroy and Steven Wofsy, atmospheric chemists at

Harvard. The two reports caused little concern because, by this time, chlorine-generating rocket fuels were no longer used. The danger of chlorine in the stratosphere seemed over. Indeed, the prestigious journal *Science* rejected a follow-up report on this danger because the editors thought that it lacked significance.

At about the same time, Rowland and Molina began to obtain troubling results from their investigations on CFCs. They discovered that a CFC molecule did not remain intact—and harmless—when bombarded by undiluted sunlight in the stratosphere. The CFC molecules broke down and released free chlorine.

Scientists were now ready to tell a disturbing story about a seemingly harmless chemical. When released at ground level, the CFC gas from spray cans and other sources remains intact and does not react with other chemicals. Slowly but surely, these gases swirl upward through the atmosphere. Some reach the stratosphere, where direct sunlight breaks up the CFC molecules. The free chlorine released from the gas then attacks and destroys many ozone molecules. As the ozone layer is depleted, more harmful ultraviolet radiation reaches the surface of the Earth.

Breaking the News

After Rowland and Molina submitted their paper for publication, Rowland took a short working holiday in Europe. He met Paul Crutzen in Vienna and disclosed the findings of his research. To ensure the accuracy of his conclusion, Rowland and Crutzen reviewed the mathematical calculations in the study. They both found the same small but important mathematical mistake. The next day, after the error had been corrected, Rowland made his presentation to a group of European colleagues. The scientists were dismayed by the news that the ozone layer was in danger.

Because of their parallel discoveries, Rowland and Crutzen now became allies in the battle to save the ozone layer from destruction. Each had contributed a major piece to the ozone puzzle. In 1970, Crutzen had proven that nitrogen oxides could deplete the ozone shield. Three years later, Rowland had found that the chlorine from CFCs was able to do the same deadly work. After Rowland's research was published in the June 1974 issue of *Nature,* the two men were deeply involved in the struggle to protect the planet.

At first, the general public was indifferent to the article by Rowland and Molina. The report by Stolarski and Cicerone had received the same lack of interest. Indeed, atmospheric scientists seemed to be the only ones concerned by the startling news. Soon, however, attitudes began to change. At a September meeting of the American Chemical Society, Rowland presented a follow-up report on the dangers of CFC. Typically, such meetings are attended by reporters from the major news media. In this case, science reporters from the *New York Times, Newsweek,* and *Time* were present. These writers are specialists in making scientific material interesting and understandable to nonscientists. Their articles are read by members of Congress and other high government officials, among others.

Sometimes, a public official responds to one of these issues by making a public comment or a short speech. In the case of Rowland's findings, the response was more vigorous. Representative Les Aspin from Wisconsin immediately submitted a bill to restrict the use of CFCs in aerosol cans. The proposed bill was assigned to a House committee for deliberation, but the session of Congress expired before hearings could be held. This meant that the bill died automatically. Therefore, a new draft of the bill had to be submitted early the following year.

The bill was resubmitted and, in early 1975, the hearings began. Many members questioned the likelihood of ozone depletion, the severity of the threat, and the government's role in such an issue. Following their usual pattern, the members of the congressional committee requested additional studies.

At the urging of Congress, the executive branch of government established the Inter-Agency Task Force to investigate the dangers of CFCs to the ozone shield. The task force, composed of members from 12 government organizations, was led by the representative of NASA.

Measurements of stratospheric ozone are made by instruments on the ground. A device using a special light meter measures the amount of dangerous radiation reaching the surface of the Earth. Low readings on the light meter indicate few harmful rays are reaching the Earth. High readings show the penetration of more radiation and mean that the ozone shield is being depleted.

To extend and verify the findings of the ground-based apparatus, NASA satellites were sent above the stratosphere. The space vehicle's instruments had been programmed to sample and analyze ozone and other atmospheric components. With few exceptions, the satellite information confirmed the findings of the ground-based instruments.

Congress soon requested the National Academy of Sciences (NAS) to assemble a special panel to review the evidence on ozone depletion. Because the NAS had already established a standing committee on air quality, the task was relatively simple. The staff of the National Research Council, a subdivision of the NAS, quickly organized the panel, and the members set to work.

In June 1975, the report of the Inter-Agency Task Force was presented to Congress. The task force confirmed the findings of Rowland and Molina. That is, their report acknowledged that chlorine was released from the CFCs in the stratosphere. Although the danger was acknowledged, many questions remained unanswered. One question concerned the whereabouts of billions of CFC molecules that had been released over the preceding years. In 1974, scientists had calculated that almost all the molecules were someplace in the atmosphere. No one knew, for example, what percentage of the CFCs had reached the high stratosphere—the level of the ozone shield. Consequently, the members of the task force could not make a final decision on the threat to human health.

Another report was released in early 1976. The review by the National Research Council (NRC) also verified the danger of CFCs. However, the NRC panel members, too, felt unable to call for the regulation of CFCs without more evidence.

Some of the legislators became tired of waiting for decisive action. They determined to employ existing laws to restrict the use of aerosols. At the time of the NRC report, the Toxic Substance Control Act was pending passage by Congress. Legislators attached a provision to the bill that would require special labeling on all canisters that contained CFCs. This act would, in effect, classify CFCs as toxic substances.

Officials of the Food and Drug Administration also utilized existing laws to restrict the use of CFCs in aerosol cans. They wrote a regulation based on the Federal Food, Drug and Cosmetic Act of 1938. The original law stipulated that all containers of toxic ingredients must carry a prominent warning. The new regulation stated clearly that CFCs were toxic and that every product containing the chemical was to be considered dangerous. Hence, the public saw warnings on hair spray, shaving cream, and, indeed, all aerosols using CFCs. In the meantime, the Environmental Protection Agency established restrictions on the import and export of CFC materials.

Industry Responses

In anticipation of a possible boycott by consumers, the manufacturers of personal care and household products lost their enthusiasm for aerosol sprays containing CFCs. Marketing specialists did not want their companies viewed as contributors to atmospheric pollution. Of equal importance, company officials knew that CFCs were not the only gas propellants that could be used in aerosol cans. They began to search for a new propellant.

On the other hand, processors of frozen foods and manufacturers of refrigeration equipment, air conditioners, and plastics were strongly opposed to any restrictions. CFCs were vitally important to their businesses and seemed irreplaceable. At first, however, these industries were not inconvenienced. The initial target was the use of CFCs in aerosol cans. When the EPA considered a ceiling on all CFC production, the industrialists joined ranks with the manufacturers who produced the CFCs. Together, they formed the Alliance for Responsible Chlorofluorocarbon Policy, a public relations and lobbying organization. The members tried to cast doubt on the science that had identified the ozone threat. They maintained that there was no hard evidence of ozone depletion.

The International Response

Everyone concerned with the CFC problem agreed that the issue was international in scope. Groups such as the Organization for Economic Cooperation and Development (OECD), the North Atlantic Treaty Organization (NATO), and several bodies associated with the United Nations added the issue to their agendas. The discussions produced much talk but little action. None of the highly industrialized countries wanted to cut back on CFC production unless all countries followed suit. All the groups looked to the United States for leadership. The situation became very uncomfortable. Powerful U.S. manufacturers produced most of the world's supply of CFCs and were unwilling to cut back or stop production. Leaders from developing countries where CFCs were produced or used in industrial processes saw the restrictions as an attempt to hamper their industrial growth.

In 1978, the United States finally passed firm regulations to ban the use of CFCs in aerosol dispensers. Sweden, Norway, and Canada passed similar laws. Political leaders of the European Economic Community (now the European Union), set goals for the reduction of CFC production. However, the target dates were far in the future and penalties for noncompliance were light.

An Uneasy Peace

In the mid-1970s, before the ban was in effect, fully 50 percent of CFCs were used in aerosol cans. To help the environment, many people had stopped using aerosols well before the ban went into effect. After the ban, the majority of people in the United States thought that the problem was solved. They were wrong. One of the problems arose because CFCs do not deteriorate under normal conditions. That means that every ounce of CFC remains in the environment. When an old air conditioner is removed to the junkyard, the metal parts deteriorate and the CFCs are released into the atmosphere. The same process occurs with empty aerosol cans, discarded refrigerators, and, indeed, every other product using CFCs.

Even though the demand for CFCs began to drop before the regulations were enacted, the market soon recovered. Almost all cars and homes were being equipped with air conditioning and CFCs were still valuable for cleaning delicate electronic parts. The world market, too, had slowed temporarily, but soon after the aerosol ban it began to grow again.

The industrialists who lobbied against the ban continued to belittle the evidence about ozone depletion. There was some uncertainty in the findings of the atmospheric chemists. The amount of CFC molecules in the stratosphere was difficult to establish. The powerful lobbyists claimed that the breakup and reformation of ozone is the result of natural processes.

Indeed, there is a rhythm to the life cycle of ozone molecules. Ozone is a fragile molecule and reverts quickly to pure oxygen. Since the sun is essential to the formation of ozone, the level drops at night and in the winter. Because the greatest intensity of sunlight is found at the equator, the highest density of ozone is found in the atmosphere above the tropics and the lowest found above the poles.

After the ban on aerosols was in effect, the general public became more complacent about the CFCs. The possibility of questionable scientific results also succeeded in calming their fears. Consequently, in 1980, when the Environmental Protection Agency officials proposed a ceiling on CFC production, the public response was unenthusiastic. U.S. Secretary of the Interior Donald Hodel joked about the issue. He was quoted as saying that people should wear sunglasses and sunscreen to guard against ultraviolet radiation rather than worry about the ozone layer.

Public opinion about ozone depletion began to shift again in 1983. One source of concern was a public scandal about the mismanagement found at the Environmental Protection Agency (EPA). The public had reason to believe that some information put out by the agency was not precisely correct and was biased in favor of large industries. EPA officials had failed to impose regulations on CFCs that had been called for by Congress. This failure had prompted a lawsuit by the National Resources Defense Council.

To regain credibility, the EPA began to work through the United Nations to arrange an international agreement to restrict CFC production. If the United States stood alone in regulating the chemical, other countries would continue production of CFCs. The worldwide threat would persist. To resolve the crises, the United Nations needed to draft an acceptable international agreement.

In 1984, members of the United Nations Environmental Program sought to restrict the production and release of CFCs. EPA delegates quickly supported this undertaking. However, west European allies of the United States were unenthusiastic about production ceilings on CFCs. Although the Americans did not want to anger the Europeans, they upheld the new U.S. regulations. A compromise agreement was prepared.

In the spring of 1985, meetings were held in Vienna, Austria, to ratify the UN agreement. Forty-three nations agreed to sign the new pact. Before the negotiations were completed, however, the arrangement to restrict CFC production was withdrawn. Delegates from western Europe and Japan had resisted the provision and the document was ineffective. The members pledged only to continue scientific research, share information, and reconvene in the future.

The outcome was frustrating to such advocates of reform as F. Sherwood Rowland. Rowland had often appeared in public forums to defend tight restrictions on CFC production. He and other environmentalists despaired that world production would not be regulated until the depletion of the ozone layer was obvious to everyone. By then, it would be too late to save the planet.

A Crisis of the Right Size

As early as 1982, advanced warnings of a new crisis were recorded by the British Antarctic Survey team. The team collected daily readings from special light meters that measured the Sun's dangerous radiation. During September and October—spring months in Antarctica—the meters registered large increases in the amount of radiant energy that reached the surface of the Earth. The team members feared that the ozone layer had thinned appreciably. At first, the team coordinator, Cambridge University scientist Joseph Farman, was highly skeptical about the accuracy of the information. Farman worried that the equipment was giving false measurements. He did not want to publicize the findings until the team was confident of its conclusion. If the scientists could not prove their contention, the negative publicity might put the survey out of business. The sponsor, the British government, would be disturbed if the scientists published an unverified account of a possible ozone crisis. At the time, British industrial interests were fighting against restrictions on CFC production.

Farman decided that he must confirm the findings before he released a report. In 1984, he compared his readings with those from an installation on the other side of the Antarctic continent. The results were almost identical. Although the report might anger the sponsors, Farman knew that he must publish his findings. On Christmas Eve 1984, he sent the document to *Nature,* the important British science journal. The article was published in May 1985.

Scientists in the United States were astonished by the news. Few had heard of Joseph Farman or the British Antarctic Survey. Cicerone and other atmospheric chemists wondered why the ozone reduction had not been detected by the NASA satellites and recorded by NASA computers.

In fact, corroborating information had been collected and reported. A researcher at the Japanese Antarctic Research Station had observed a monthlong record of ozone depletion. In 1984, the Japanese scientist reported his findings at a small research meeting in Greece. The significance of this information was not recognized by those at the meeting. Ironically, the members included F. Sherwood Rowland.

Both humans and computers have an imperfect ability to analyze information. Scientists soon discovered NASA's computer problem. The computer had been programmed to analyze information sent from the satellites. However, to avoid false readings, the computer was programmed to ignore measurements that greatly deviated from the average. Although the low ozone count over Antarctica had been properly recorded by the instruments, the unusual measurements had been disregarded by the computer and had not appeared on the printouts. When the satellite readings were reevaluated, scientists learned that a hole in the ozone layer had first appeared in 1979. By 1984, the hole had grown to be the size of the United States. The level of ozone within the hole was even lower than the atmospheric chemists had predicted. They had anticipated a 15 percent decrease in ozone but the measurements showed fully 50 percent—an awesome drop.

No Retreat

In summer 1986, news of the ozone hole was reported by the media. Even with this evidence, the CFC manufacturers did not admit defeat. Their publicists stated that the ozone hole was a temporary abnormality. They were convinced that the next set of readings—due in September and October—would prove that the ozone layer was intact.

Shortly after the British and Japanese findings were made public, the National Oceanographic and Atmospheric Administration (NOAA) organized an expedition to the Antarctic. The group arrived during August—late winter in the Southern Hemisphere.

They recorded ozone data during the South Pole's spring months of September and October. Unfortunately for the manufacturers, the expedition gathered information that proved the reappearance of the hole. Fortunately for the environmentalists, news of the Antarctic hole captured the attention of the public. NASA published impressive diagrams based on measurements recorded by the satellites. The images made it clear that something very strange was happening to the ozone layer. The public wanted immediate action.

The manufacturers continued to claim that chlorine from CFCs did not cause the hole. They maintained that more research was needed to resolve the issue. Indeed, atmospheric

Ralph Cicerone laid out the steps by which each chlorine atom could destroy a large number of ozone molecules. (Courtesy of Ralph Cicerone)

chemists such as Ralph Cicerone were also cautious. Cicerone wanted another year of observations before making a final decision about the ozone-CFC problem.

The United Nations Comes to the Fore

Even before reports of the Antarctic ozone hole in summer 1986, the UN Environmental Program and the U.S. Environmental Protection Agency were holding a series of meetings. These technical and political discussion groups met in Leesburg, Virginia. They drafted severe regulations to limit CFC production. With this in mind, manufacturers conceded that some regulations were necessary. Undoubtedly, this decision reflected their self-interest. The industrialists knew that a substitute for

CFC would eventually be found. Each hoped to discover and market the replacement.

Another important conference began in September 1987. The UN Environmental Program was scheduled to convene in Montreal, Canada. Some U.S. delegates were still undecided. However, George Bush, then U.S. vice president, advocated an international agreement to suppress the production of CFCs. The United States was now a leader in the movement. Even so, the conference soon bogged down. To avoid the embarrassment of a totally unproductive meeting, last-minute compromises were made. After the revisions were completed, the first international environmental agreement was signed by 57 countries in September 1987. Skeptics remarked that the most productive outcome about the agreement was the decision to continue research on ozone depletion.

The Big Push in the Antarctic

While the Montreal meetings were under way, a second and larger Antarctic expedition was being organized by NOAA with technical collaboration from NASA. The leaders of the team of scientists was Susan Solomon. The scientists were given the support of light meters on the ground, satellite observations overhead, and a very high-altitude NASA research plane, the ER-2. The research plane was scheduled to fly into the ozone hole at an altitude of 60,000 feet (18,000 m). The flight was dangerous because the ER-2 has a single engine and had never been flown near the South Pole, where temperatures drop to –130 degrees Fahrenheit (–90 degrees Celsius). Although the instruments did not work properly on the first flight, the second flight was a total success.

By using information gathered from the ground, the satellite, and the plane, Solomon's team successfully measured the chlorine molecules in the Antarctic ozone hole. All of the readings were high. In fact, the concentration of chlorine was 300 times greater than expected. The connection between chlorine and the ozone hole was firmly established.

Ironically, an explanation for the Antarctic hole had been proposed by Ralph Cicerone shortly before this discovery. He had mathematically demonstrated that chlorine molecules in the stratosphere could attach themselves to microscopic ice crystals. When the Antarctic spring sun reached these crystals, the ice would melt and the chlorine would be released. It could promptly attack the ozone molecules. The only possible source of chlorine was the CFCs. Ultimately, Solomon would win the Blue Earth Award and Cicerone would be elected president of the National Academy of Sciences.

Susan Solomon (pictured with President Bill Clinton) led the team that discovered why the ozone hole was seasonal. (Courtesy of the National Science and Technology Medals Foundation)

The ER-2 was flown near the South Pole in extremely low temperatures to determine how much free chlorine was present at stratospheric levels. (Courtesy of the National Aeronautics and Space Administration)

Final Victory

The publicity about the Antarctic ozone hole solidified public opinion in favor of restricting CFC production. Most people thought that CFC manufacturers must give up their battle against regulations. Undaunted, the industrialists continued to deny that CFCs were depleting the ozone layer. However, their own industrial chemists recognized that the struggle was useless. The public would become hostile if the companies did not accept the facts. In mid-March, 1988, the main U.S. producer of CFCs announced that production would soon cease.

More than seven years later, on October 11, 1995, F. Sherwood Rowland, his partner, Mario Molina, and their European collaborator, Paul Crutzen, were awarded the Nobel Prize for chemistry in a ceremony in Stockholm, Sweden. For 20 years, Rowland had spoken to indifferent or skeptical audiences about the ozone crises. The Nobel Prize was a fitting recognition for his diligence.

The political leaders of the world quickly responded to the explanation of the chemical processes causing ozone depletion by putting forth firm new public policies. For example, in the United States the administrators of the EPA announced a total

This Arctic research station has many functions—one of which is to give advance warning if the ozone level at the North Pole begins to decline, as it has done at the South Pole. (Courtesy of the National Weather Service)

ban on CFC production in 1996. Top officials of other industrialized nations followed suit, but the collective view was that such a ban was not urgently needed for the less industrialized nations. The less industrialized countries, such as Pakistan and Bolivia, produced only a small fraction of the quantities of CFCs produced in Europe, Japan, and North America, but nevertheless their industries such as refrigerator manufacturing needed cheap CFCs if they were to grow into profitable businesses.

Carryovers

In spite of the total ban on CFC production and restrictions on CFC importation within the industrialized countries, three significant problems remain into the 21st century. The first matter is not a problem for science—it is a problem for law enforcement. Specifically, CFCs are being smuggled into the United States from those countries that were allowed to continue their manufacture. Profits for such endeavors are substantial. CFCs can be produced in a developing country for about $1.00 a pound. The commodity can be sold in the United States for around $20.00 a pound. While thousands of pounds of CFC material have been intercepted at the borders, the traffic continues. Even though production of CFCs is due to stop in all countries in 2010, CFCs will still be plentiful. Every air conditioner and refrigerator made before the year 2000 has CFCs in its cooling system. The CFCs in such equipment can be captured and resold. In fact there is no legal penalty to do so. There is even a net gain for the environment because much of the recycled CFCs will be put back into closed systems when used to replenish the material in, for example, a damaged air conditioner. Meanwhile, however, CFCs smuggled into the United States can be sold in a thriving black market where they are disguised as recycled material.

The second issue does have a science aspect. Farmers—mainly in western states—use a material called methyl bromide to control infestations of underground worms and beetle larvae. The methyl bromide is an ozone-depleting agent, and researchers have found it in the stratosphere.

The methyl bromide gas is injected into the soil from pressurized tanks. Environmentalists have sought to have its use banned. The chemical is highly toxic to animals and humans as well as being a strong ozone depleting agent. As a toxic material, it could be banned as an ecological hazard. New regulations, supported by statute, were supposed to go into effect in 2000. However, the legislation was amended in the House of Representatives so that agricultural use was extended to 2010, albeit with some safeguards for people who live near the fields being treated. Some substitute compounds have been developed, but scientists need to perfect a more economical alternative.

The third problem is that the substitutes for the CFCs that were introduced with some acclaim in the 1990s are serious greenhouse gases. The initial substitutes for the CFCs are quite close in structure to the CFCs. The main difference is that the substitutes have two carbon atoms per molecule while the CFCs have only one. Radiation reflection tests indicate that the substitutes are stronger greenhouse gases than carbon dioxide. A new round of research and development is needed to find materials that can be used in the same way the CFCs were used but are not toxic, do not deplete the stratospheric ozone layer, and do not contribute to global warming.

On the plus side, the CFC episode raised many new questions about the possible presence of a variety of chemicals in the upper atmosphere. The CFC molecules are heavier than air, nevertheless, they are found at all levels of the atmosphere including the stratosphere. That observation raised the possibility that other chemicals could be transported to the upper atmosphere by normal air currents. Consequently, in the

Dr. Nicola Blake, a member of F. Sherwood Rowland's research team, checking on the instruments for determining the level of trace materials— including chlorine compounds—at stratospheric altitudes (Courtesy of the National Aeronautics and Space Administration)

1990s, NASA sponsored a study of the upper atmosphere whereby samples taken at altitude by rigorous methods would be tested for the presence of 46 different chemicals. Included in the tests were detectors for 13 molecules that contain either chlorine or bromine. Coincidentally, F. Sherwood Rowland headed the project, with a research staff from the University of California at San Diego. The idea is to avoid future surprises, such as the unexpected link between the CFCs and ozone depletion in the stratosphere.

10
Breathing Particles

A human adult usually inhales about 3,400 gallons of air in a day. Given that degree of exposure, it is not surprising that the lungs can be the site of a variety of disorders. These include various forms of cancer, viral and bacterial infections, emphysema, and asthma.

The causal agents for some lung conditions are well established. For example, tobacco is now proven to be a factor in many types of cancer, including cancer of the lungs. Plant pollen has a well-established role in allergic reactions that affect the lungs. Although some causes of lung disorders are shrouded in ambiguity and uncertainty, it is true that air pollution is an aggravating factor in almost every case.

One source of localized air pollution is asbestos dust. Asbestos is a mineral that is obtained by underground mining. Some forms of asbestos rock yield fine, long fibers that can be twisted into a yarn and woven into fireproof, asbestos cloth. As early as the second century C.E., Roman merchants shipped their asbestos cloth to central Asia and bartered for Chinese silk and other commodities. Roman officials of that ancient period recognized a connection between lung disorders and working with asbestos. However, since fireproof cloth could command high prices, officials were uninterested in interfering with the production of the product. The mining, fiber extraction, spinning, and weaving of asbestos continued to be unregulated.

For hundreds of years after the fall of the Roman Empire, asbestos and asbestos products continued to be articles of trade but were minor elements in European commerce. Because of its relative unimportance, the medical profession paid little attention to health problems resulting from asbestos exposure. This situation began to change in the mid-1800s when large quantities of high-grade asbestos ore were discovered in Canada. As it became available, the industrial exploitation of this mineral proceeded rapidly. The ancient technologies of asbestos manufacture were modernized, and many new applications were developed. The uses eventually included such products as brake pads for automobiles and insulation for industrial and domestic buildings.

As Europe and North America entered a mature industrial age, the value of asbestos in manufacturing and construction grew steadily. With the expansion of asbestos mining and the increase in industrial uses, the link between exposure to asbestos dust and lung disease became more apparent. By the 1930s, asbestos particles were found in scar tissue from the lungs of people who had died of congestive lung disorder. During the 1940s, public health professionals began to note a correlation between a worker's exposure to asbestos and the presence of lung cancer. This connection was difficult to establish because the cancer often remained undetected until long after the victim had stopped working in an asbestos dust environment. Therefore, the only cases that showed a clear connection were those found in patients currently employed by an asbestos industry. Another complication in assessing blame soon became apparent. Many of the lung cancer victims both worked with asbestos and smoked tobacco, so the causal factor of the cancerous condition was difficult to isolate. Medical researchers now believe that exposure to the two dangerous substances—asbestos dust and tobacco—amplify the possibility of being stricken with lung cancer.

To further confuse matters, not all forms of asbestos are equally dangerous. The long fibers that are spun and woven are relatively benign because they are heavier and less likely to be airborne. Researchers determined that the most unsafe environment is one in which the air is filled with microscopic particles of asbestos dust. Although this type of disease-causing dust is found in many workplaces where asbestos is present, by far the most hazardous jobs are those in the mining of asbestos and in the manufacturing of asbestos pipes. In these industries, asbestos powder—a very fine, easily airborne asbestos dust—is used as a raw material.

In spite of the apparent connection between asbestos and lung disease, the use of asbestos has not been explicitly banned in the United States. Laws have been brought to congressional committees but never passed. Regulations proposed by various government agencies have been difficult to enforce. However, some sanctions have proven successful even in the absence of laws that specifically prohibit the mining or use of asbestos. The Occupational Safety and Health Administration (OSHA) began to assert limits on worker exposure to asbestos particles in the 1960s. In the following decades, however, the main influence has been from civil actions in the courts. Firms that used asbestos as a raw material or as an insulating material have been forced to pay damage claims to hundreds of workers who suffer from lung diseases—particularly cancers. The workers' claims have been substantiated (proved true) by the results of a series of studies. The research provided an accumulation of evidence that showed asbestos was a powerful causal factor in lung disease. These results led judges and juries to rule against firms using asbestos. Consequently, use has steadily declined. Activist groups, too, have had some local impact on the problem. For example, in the 1990s, activists helped defeat a Montana congressman who had promoted the continued mining and use of asbestos.

In 1973, more than 700,000 tons of asbestos were used by manufacturing and construction industries in the United States.

Today, almost all asbestos mining in the United States has ceased, and the industrial use of asbestos has been reduced to about 15,000 tons a year. Meanwhile, the Environmental Protection Agency (EPA) has been able to impose even stronger regulations to limit the use of asbestos where children live or attend school. The involvement of medical researchers, the legal system, agencies such as OSHA and the EPA, and dedicated activists all contributed to the decrease in asbestos usage. The experiences of these groups have provided a basic precedent for the regulation of other particulate materials.

Other Particles

Coal dust was a major factor in lung disease until the 1980s. The symptoms presented by coal miners were called "Black Lung Disease." Autopsies of the victims revealed that their lungs had been blackened with the absorbed coal dust, and soon this particulate became almost as notorious as asbestos. Silicosis, a noncancerous disease with similar symptoms, is another ailment that affects miners. Autopsies of these victims exposed a disturbing—although less dramatic—picture: lungs grey with stone dust rather than blackened by coal.

Further research on lung diseases included autopsies of lung cancer victims who did not work in high risk occupations. Microscopic examination often revealed extremely small particles embedded in the lung tissue. By the 1990s, medical evidence pointed to all very fine airborne particles as a threat to human health. Apparently, larger particles—the size of a pinpoint—can be expelled by the lung's defensive processes such as normal coughing. Small particles, less than one-100th the diameter of a human hair, become so tightly embedded that they are actually inside the cells of lung tissue.

In the 1960s, some atmospheric scientists said that visible smoke was not particularly harmful—only a bit of soot, carbon

A smoky urban street scene, circa 1955 (Courtesy of the Environmental Protection Agency)

dioxide, and water vapor were present in ordinary smoke—including the black plumes from diesel engines. Scientists have since learned that even the ordinary smoke from wood fires contains particles that could be a threat to human health. It did not take a long time to discover that smoke—regardless of the fuel—contained many such particles. However, regulation of exposure to smoke presented a different set of difficulties.

Smoke comes from many sources—some quite small and innocuous, such as a wood-burning fireplace. Regulatory agents were reluctant to ban such fires and sought to identify sources that contributed a disproportionate quantity of particulate material to the atmosphere. Some attention was directed to the usual suspects: power plants that used coal and other fossil fuels. Eventually, local and state governments issued bans on burning leaves and other yard trash and a widely pursued practice—enjoyed by some families—had to be abandoned.

As the public health picture became clearer, Congress amended the Clean Air Act that had been enacted in 1970. The amendments directed the Environmental Protection Agency to set specific standards for particulate pollution as limits on the number of particles in a given size range per cubic yard of air. When the standards were published in 1992, environmental activists and public health advocates were not satisfied. In 1994, the American Lung Association brought suit against the EPA in an attempt to set more stringent standards. This widely publicized move caught the attention of some senators, and hearings were scheduled. These hearings allowed both public health and industry representatives to express their concerns. Public health professionals generally sought tighter restrictions on emissions while industry representatives wanted more leeway. In 2002, the EPA published new guidelines on particulate emissions. However, by August 2004, no new regulations were in place, and reviews were still underway. Most new regulations have been enacted by the separate states.

Research now points to very small particles as a dangerous threat to human health. Originally, attention was focused on particles with an average diameter of 10 microns. A single micron is exceedingly small—32 10-micron particles would fit on a pin point. The newer findings suggest that particles in the range of 2.5 microns and smaller are even more dangerous. Additional studies have shown that individuals suffering from lung disorders are especially affected by particulate pollution. Their medical condition means that they are less able to defend themselves from the danger of particulates. People with healthy lungs can easily recover from acute exposure instances, such as hiking through a dust storm. The condition of those whose lungs are already irritated by asthma or emphysema is quickly worsened by such exposure.

When public health scientists saw this connection, a question arose about the fatalities attributed to particle pollution. Was it possible that those who died were so infirm that they would have died in a few days or hours whether exposed to polluted air or not? Further studies indicate that while there was some "harvesting" of the infirm, the actual incidences of such deaths were small.

In testimony before the Senate Environment and Public Works Committee in 2002, representatives of the electric power industry pointed to the fact that all forms of harmful, smokestack emissions were declining and that the proportion of particulates from other sources—such as vehicular traffic or diesel engines—was increasing. Representatives of engine manufacturers agreed that diesel engines were notorious sources of particulates. However, they argued that because diesel engines yielded superior mileage compared to gasoline engines, the

Dust from windblown soil can contain microscopic particles that are injurious to lung tissue. (Courtesy of the Agricultural Research Service)

benefits outweighed the penalties. Also, they noted that removing the particles from diesel exhaust by adding filters and other more complicated equipment would cost diesel users thousands of dollars per engine.

The atmospheric scientists who testified at these hearings warned that even though particle concentrations could be measured so that compliance with emission standards could be determined, the measurements lacked precision because the actual chemical composition of the particles was so varied. Some particles were like very fine sand—essentially silicon compounds. Other particles were formed of elemental carbon, like soot, or other organic materials like unburned gasoline droplets. Other particles were formed of molecules that included the basic pollutants such as the oxides of nitrogen and sulfur that came from burning fossil fuels.

Despite the prospects of incurring some major costs and the fact that the knowledge about particle pollution was incomplete, the message from the congressional hearings was that the risk to human health was serious and that tighter regulations were in order. By the turn of the century in 2000, regulations limiting the emissions from diesel-powered trucks were established. Fortunately, the cost of cleaning the diesel exhaust was lowered by the development of advanced designs of catalytic converters for diesel engines. Also, engineers discovered that emissions could be reduced by using cleaner fuels, including vegetable oils rather than petroleum oil, mixtures including grain alcohol, and even small amounts of water.

The engineering advances made the prospect of tighter standards seem more reasonable, so the EPA specified precise limits to the amount of particulate material that could be present in the atmosphere. Measurement of the degree of pollution was generally localized in cities or downwind of major sources such as steel mills. However, the principal political jurisdictions that are asked to comply with these standards are the states. In 2004, pollution surveys done by the EPA indicated that 29 states and the District of Columbia were not in compliance with the standards.

Each state and many minor jurisdictions such as cities or counties have their own environmental regulations, including restrictions on the release of particulates. Most follow the lines laid down by the federal regulations—though some are more rigorous. Enforcement at the local level is usually in the hands of civilian inspectors. Violators are cited but are usually given some leeway in responding to a complaint. The most common form of punishment is a court order to cease the polluting behavior. Only after other options have been exhausted is firm legal action taken. Then the polluter is brought into court, and a fine can result. Only the most extreme cases result in criminal proceedings and a possible jail sentence.

In the meantime, the EPA has continued to expand the range of regulation of particulate pollution. In 2004, all off-road and stationary diesel-powered equipment was brought under the air quality rules. This means that heavy-duty farm machines and stationary engines that drive pumps or provide emergency power generation must have particle filters or use special fuels or both. While compliance with the regulations governing exposure to particles will not always be prompt or complete, the combined weight of the public health authorities, the EPA, and the workplace monitors such as the Occupational Safety and Health Administration seems likely to reduce the exposure of vulnerable individuals to reasonable levels within the next few years.

11
Global Warming

Many scientists believe that the Earth is getting warmer. The warming trend is thought to be the result of a condition called the greenhouse effect. Although the ozone layer screens out most of the Sun's harmful ultraviolet rays, atmospheric gases allow the Sun's beneficial radiant energy to reach the surface of the Earth. When the Sun's radiant energy reaches the surface, it acts to warm whatever it touches. As soon as the warming begins, the heat energy starts radiating back into the cooler atmosphere. In an apparent contradiction, the same gases that allow the Sun's rays to enter the atmosphere also block much of the newly generated heat from ascending into outer space. Indeed, the gases in the air reflect the heat back toward the ground. This allows the planet to retain warmth and support life. The gases act in much the same manner as the glass walls and roof of a gardener's greenhouse. They allow sunlight in, but help keep the heat from escaping. Thus, this process is called the greenhouse effect.

This effect is noticeable on warm late spring or early summer days. After a clear, bright, sunny day, temperatures in the Middle Atlantic states can easily reach 80 degrees Fahrenheit (27 degrees Celsius). If the skies remain clear at night, the temperature will fall into the 60s (16 degrees Celsius) before dawn. The clear night sky allows much of the surface heat to radiate into space. However, if clouds roll in during the evening, the night will remain warm. Temperatures will fall only into the

70s (21 degrees Celsius). The clouds serve as a blanket—or the roof of a greenhouse. They block the heat radiating from the ground and reflect it back toward the surface of the Earth.

Water as a Greenhouse Gas

Water vapor and carbon dioxide gas are chiefly responsible for the greenhouse effect. Whether in the form of clouds or as an invisible gas, water vapor accounts for about 75 percent of this condition. Water vapor, along with nitrogen and oxygen, is one of the three most abundant atmospheric gases. Therefore, it is not too surprising that water vapor is the most effective greenhouse gas. However, carbon dioxide (CO_2), which accounts for only .0003 of the Earth's atmosphere, is the second most important greenhouse gas.

Water vapor and carbon dioxide contribute to the greenhouse effect in different ways. The far greater quantity of water vapor molecules is more effective at blocking the heat from escaping into outer space. However, the carbon dioxide molecules are more efficient at reflecting the heat back toward the surface of the Earth so that the much smaller amount of CO_2 makes a significant contribution. Together, the two gases account for more than 95 percent of the greenhouse effect.

Recently, scientists have proven that the level of atmospheric carbon dioxide is on the rise. Therefore, the greater number of carbon dioxide molecules in the blanket of atmospheric gases will increase both the heat-blocking and heat-reflective ability of the gas. Less heat will be able to escape into deep space.

The anticipated increase of CO_2 will aggravate the greenhouse problem. A warming trend will lead to a more rapid evaporation of water from the world's oceans. This will send more water vapor into the atmosphere. The presence of more water vapor will improve the heat retention of the atmospheric blanket. The greenhouse effect will increase, and the warming trend will continue at a faster pace.

Carbon Dioxide

In spring 1755, a Scottish scientist named Joseph Black identified carbon dioxide as a gas with a specific molecular construction. More than 100 years later, in 1896, Svante Arrhenius, a Swedish physical chemist, performed research that led to important discoveries about CO_2. Arrhenius had spent many years investigating electrical conductivity and found that CO_2 is a good insulator. Toward the end of his career, his interests expanded, and he sought to explain the ice ages. Arrhenius's new studies showed that carbon dioxide acts as an insulator to help maintain the Earth's climate. In other words, CO_2 helps retain the Sun's warmth. Arrhenius concluded that an increased amount of CO_2 had contributed to the warmer temperatures that melted the glaciers and caused the end of the Ice Age. The idea that carbon dioxide could influence the Earth's climate was not easily accepted by his fellow scientists. Subsequent research, however, verified his theory. During the last 15 years of his life, he shared his knowledge and love of chemistry by producing science books for children and nonscientists. Before his death in 1927, Arrhenius was honored with the Nobel Prize for chemistry and other important awards.

Too Much Carbon Dioxide

In 1938, a British mining engineer, George Callendar, completed a 10-year study of the Earth's climate. After a careful analysis of his temperature readings, Callendar concluded that the information revealed a general warming trend. The British engineer knew of Arrhenius's report and was convinced this trend indicated an increase of atmospheric CO_2. Most scientists were skeptical of his conclusion. They saw no hard evidence of an increase in carbon dioxide.

By 1958, the warming trend and the CO_2 problem had become more apparent. Scientists from 70 countries participated in a series of meetings called the International Geophysical Year—a project that lasted for 18 months. The participants hoped to establish a set of basic measurements on global climate factors such as temperature, rainfall, and atmospheric carbon dioxide. All future measurements of climate factors would be compared to these basic measurements, and any significant changes would be easy to detect. Roger Revelle, the head of the Scripps Institute of Oceanography at La Jolla, California, led the planning groups.

Revelle and a colleague, Hans Suess, were especially concerned about the possible increase in atmospheric carbon dioxide. They began to investigate whether the oceans would be able to absorb a greater amount of this gas. The scientists hoped that increased atmospheric carbon dioxide would be used by sea creatures to manufacture their shells. However, the scientists found that the oceans and the sea creatures were incapable of removing much additional carbon dioxide. Consequently, Revelle and Suess stressed the necessity of establishing an accurate baseline to monitor the increasing amounts of CO_2 in the atmosphere.

This task was assigned to Charles Keeling. Keeling had designed a delicate instrument that accurately measures CO_2. The sensitive device detects a change of one molecule of carbon dioxide per million molecules of air. In order to establish the baseline measurements of CO_2, Keeling installed one of his instruments on the slopes of Mauna Loa in Hawaii. The site is far from any industrial activity, and the daily measurements were free of contamination.

The CO_2 readings from Mauna Loa have become classic scientific data. The records show a saw-toothed progression that began in 1960 with 320 parts of CO_2 per million and increased to more than 370 parts per million by 2004. The Keeling Curve is undisputed evidence that the amount of CO_2 is growing and that the rate of growth increases every year.

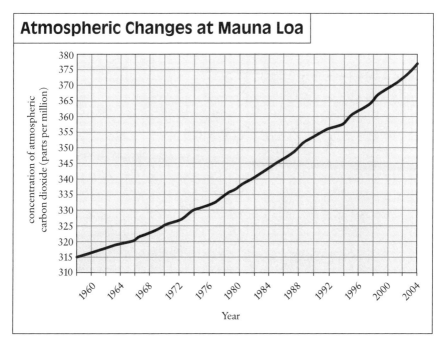

Atmospheric Changes at Mauna Loa

Observations made by Keeling at Mauna Loa show the gradual increase in the amount of carbon dioxide in the atmosphere.

General Effects

Scientists agree that global warming will not be uniform around the Earth. The greatest warming will occur near the North and South Poles and the least at the equator. The areas between the poles and the equator will show a gradual and intermediate rise in temperature.

Specialists in many countries are studying this greenhouse effect to determine how fast temperatures will rise and how this change will affect life on Earth. Whether the temperature rise is rapid or gradual, millions of people will be affected.

The economies of many industrialized countries depend on electric power manufactured by steam turbines. Coal, oil, and natural gas—the fossil fuels—produce most of the steam.

Unfortunately, all fossil fuels create carbon dioxide as one of their waste products. Coal is the worst offender. To make each kilowatt of electricity, coal produces 10 percent more carbon dioxide than oil and twice as much as natural gas.

If the burning of coal is restricted, the cost of electricity will rise because coal is cheaper than oil or natural gas. If the price of electricity increases, luxuries such as air conditioning may be restricted to the rich. If the electric companies try to maintain existing prices by cutting back on production, power fail-

David Keeling receiving the Science Medal from President George W. Bush. (Courtesy of the National Science Foundation)

ures will be more frequent. Brownouts, caused by temporarily reducing the amount of electricity, will become commonplace. In short, the lifestyle of countless individuals will become less pleasant because of restrictions on fossil fuels. This possibility is unacceptable to most citizens. Scientists, engineers, and environmentalists are seeking alternative methods to generate electric power without increasing atmospheric carbon dioxide.

Specific Effects

If global warming happens quickly, a serious consequence could be the breakup and partial melting of the polar ice caps. The melt water would cause ocean levels to rise and flood low-lying coastal areas. Unfortunately, many of the world's richest and most populous cities are located near bodies of water. In industrialized countries, the main problem will be property loss. New York City in the United States and Amsterdam in the Netherlands are prominent examples of wealthy coastal cities. In the less industrialized countries, flooding will cause many casualties, destruction of buildings, reduction in agricultural land, and consequent food shortages. Poor cities such as Chittagong in Bangladesh, located on the Bay of Bengal, will experience major problems.

If the sea level rises slowly, human adaptability will be able to minimize the loss of life. However, the loss of property will be extensive. Unless enormous dikes are built, such as those in Holland, valuable buildings and agricultural land will become unusable.

Other Effects

The U.S. Department of Energy has funded studies to determine the effect of a warming trend on human health, agriculture, forestry, and fishing. In the matter of human health, diseases prevalent in tropical or semitropical regions could become commonplace in northern areas. For example, malaria might someday be a health problem in countries that are now too cold to support the tropical *Anopheles* mosquito responsible for transmitting the illness.

If winters in Canada and northern United States become milder, some illnesses such as colds and flu could be alleviated. Of greater importance is the fact that fewer people die of heat-related problems than exposure to extreme cold. Therefore, the warming trend would benefit the poorest and most vulnerable segments of society.

In agriculture, a warmer climate and an increase in carbon dioxide might seem to be a benefit for humankind. A carbon-dioxide–enriched environment causes many plants to grow more rapidly and to a larger size. Growing seasons would lengthen. Land that produces a single yearly crop might be able to grow two successive crops. However, two possibilities cloud this happy prospect. First, soil conditions change from one region to another. Both soil and climate are responsible for the highly productive corn-growing regions of Indiana, Illinois, and Iowa. A warming trend might shift the best growing conditions into northern states such as Michigan. The soil in those states, however, is not as well suited for the cultivation of corn. The yield of this important crop would suffer.

Adverse effects would result if a climate change caused a difference in the pattern of rainfall. Less rainfall could transform productive growing areas into deserts. If the water flowing in the Colorado River and its tributaries decreased in volume, the consequences could be disastrous. Millions of people depend on this river to provide crop irrigation, drinking water, and recreation. Parts of the Southwest, such as southern California, would suffer greatly from any change in the fragile river system.

Global warming would affect forests. Each species of tree grows best in a specific soil and temperature range. Although tree populations would be less affected than farm crops by changing weather conditions, some tree species might become extinct.

The fishing industry would experience extensive changes from a warming climate. In major saltwater fishing areas, the food chain is supported by tiny, aquatic, one-celled plants and animals called plankton. Plankton thrive in relatively cold, nutrient-rich water that has risen to the surface from the depths of the ocean. If the ocean waters become warmer, the numbers and vigor of the small creatures could be reduced. Smaller fish would have less to eat. Large, edible fish would decline in numbers because their food supply would diminish. The fishing industry fears that this possibility might cause the extinction of many popular favorites, and the amount of fish in the human diet would decrease.

El Niño

A study of natural climate and weather variations such as El Niño gives scientists some understanding of man-made environmental problems such as the greenhouse effect. El Niño is a strange meteorological condition that recurs every two to seven years and affects the climate of the entire world. It usually develops off the coast of Peru in the month of November and reaches its peak in December near Christmastime. Indeed, El Niño is the Spanish expression for the Christ child. El Niño has been noted by Peruvian farmers and fishermen for many decades because its arrival signals a dramatic change in the fish population and an equally dramatic increase in rainfall. Curiously, this peculiar weather condition stimulated little scientific interest or investigation until fairly recently.

Normally, strong trade winds blow the warm surface water away from the coast of central South America and across the Pacific Ocean toward Asia. The enormous volume of water that is swept westward actually causes the ocean level off Asia to measure two feet higher than that off central South America. Near the Peruvian coast, cold, nutrient-rich water rises up from the deep ocean to replace the water swept westward by the winds.

When El Niño comes, these strong, westerly winds weaken, and the warm surface water flows back toward the coast of central South America. The water levels of the eastern and western coasts of the Pacific are equalized. Along the coast of Peru, the normal upsurge of cold water is inhibited by the presence of warm surface water from the mid-Pacific. Peruvian fishing is immediately affected because the surface water does not carry nutrients to the coastal fishing grounds.

In the early 1920s, Sir Gilbert Walker, a British scientist, began investigating weather conditions in the western Pacific between Australia and Indonesia. At first, Walker's work indicated that atmospheric pressure in the region was uncommonly stable. He found that high atmospheric pressure is usually recorded along the southwestern rim of the Pacific and low pressure along the southeastern rim. Soon, however, Walker realized that every few years, the pressure readings are reversed during the months of November and December. During those months, low atmospheric pressure is recorded in the southwestern Pacific and high pressure in the southeast. Walker called the seesaw phenomenon the Southern Oscillation. No one associated these meteorological findings with the strange rhythmic occurrence of El Niño. It was not until 1966 that Jacob Bjerknes perceived the connection.

Jacob Bjerknes and his father, Vilhelm, are famous for the mathematical and graphical representations used in weather forecasting. In the early 1940s, Jacob Bjerknes traveled to the United States from Scandinavia to give a series of lectures. During that time, the German army invaded and quickly conquered his native country of Norway. Bjerknes was trapped in the United States. He was invited to join the faculty at the University of California at Los Angeles and soon founded the Department of Atmospheric Science there.

In the early 1960s, Bjerknes was engaged in a long-term study of the relationship between the oceans and the atmosphere. While analyzing conditions off the coast of Peru, he noted a recurring event. In most years, high barometric pressure is prevalent during November and December. During these years, strong prevailing winds blow from east to west. However, every few years, the barometric pressure during those same months is dramatically reduced, and the winds blow from west to east. Local fishing and farming are disrupted, and strange weather conditions are reported.

Jacob Bjerknes was a brilliant weather forecaster from Norway who founded the Department of Atmospheric Science at the University of California at Los Angeles. He was the first person to understand the workings of the El Niño effect. (Courtesy of Eugene Rasmusson)

Bjerknes was familiar with Sir Gilbert Walker's research on atmosphere pressure in the western Pacific. He realized that his observations along the eastern coast of the ocean echoed the cyclic pressure changes recorded by Walker. El Niño was recognized as a worldwide phenomenon.

The impact of El Niño is large and varied. Scientists believe that an investigation of these changes will reveal possible consequences of future global warming. Strategies that modify the adverse results of El Niño can be used to modify the greenhouse effect. For example, rainfall in the usually semiarid zone near the west coast of Peru increases dramatically during El

Niño years. Improved forecasting now informs farmers of the upcoming weather. To benefit from El Niño's rain, they can cultivate a moisture-loving plant such as rice that season. Similar variations in agricultural practices will be necessary to survive a global climate change.

The fishing industry must also expect disruptions during El Niño. Catches of cold-water fish, such as sardines and anchovies, decline. However, other popular seafoods, like scallops, are more abundant. In 1997, the sea off California experienced a profusion of nonnative, warm-water fish. Those who engage in sports fishing were overjoyed by the prospect of catching large numbers of unusual fish. Presumably, the effects of El Niño were responsible for currents of warm water that brought the fish. Perhaps, displaced fish will be one of the results of a global warming.

Many effects of El Niño are damaging to people and crops. In some areas, excessive rain causes temporary lakes to form in low-lying land. The standing water expands the breeding grounds of the *Anopheles* mosquito and adds to the risk of malaria. The rains also promote the growth of wild plants that provide abundant food for destructive insects. Insects such as grasshoppers soon show an increase in both size and numbers. El Niño is responsible for other unusual weather patterns. Expected rainy seasons are sometimes replaced by drought. This weather condition causes crop failures, reduces the availability of drinking water, and permits forest and brush fires in the western Pacific islands.

Diagnosis and Predictions

Climatologists are determined to establish a firm timetable for global warming. To achieve this goal, they use mathematical models to simulate future climate conditions. Climate models are similar to—but less exact than—those used to predict the weather. Weather models are designed to predict a few days of weather conditions affecting an area of a few hundred square miles while climate models are designed to predict decades of climate conditions affecting huge segments of the Earth's surface. Climate models use grids (similar to those found in graph paper) to plot both horizontal and vertical information. Depending on the type of computer, each side of a horizontal grid represents from 60 to 200 miles (96–320 km) of the Earth's surface. A vertical grid represents 20 successive layers of atmosphere—beginning at the Earth's surface and continuing up to the stratosphere. When the horizontal grid is combined with the vertical grid, the computer screen shows a cube-like projection.

Using the grid framework, climate models can incorporate dozens of factors, such as the prevalence of carbon dioxide, temperatures at various levels, and prevailing wind directions. Some factors are difficult to portray. Temperature exchanges between the oceans and the atmosphere have been especially complicated. Scientists believe that as some climate changes begin, changes may also take place in the paths of ocean currents. Thus, ocean currents may affect climate and climate may affect ocean currents. Recently, climate modeling has made it possible to portray the "coupling" (the linkage or joining together) of oceanic effects and climate change.

Other factors plotted on the grids include the intensity of the Sun's radiation. The intensity varies from week to week, month to month, year to year, and millennium to millennium. Since the Earth was formed, this and other changeable conditions have caused the worldwide climate to vary in a nearly cyclic fashion.

Some climate cycles continue for hundreds of thousands of years. Climatologists can detect the effects of these long, slow changes by studying the gases trapped in ice cores. Such cores are extracted from the permanent ice shield of Greenland in the Northern Hemisphere and from Antarctica in the Southern Hemisphere. In 2004, Russian and American scientists removed ice cores that were formed 750,000 years ago and in 2005, they hope to extract cores formed 1 million years ago.

Scientists assert that our present-day climate is due to a brief period of relative warmth which is taking place in the midst of a comparatively short ice age. The present ice age peaked about 20,000 years ago when glaciers covered most of North America and northern Europe. Most climatologists believe that the warming period will end soon and that the Earth's climate will slowly return to the current ice age.

In contrast to long, slow cycles, some cycles last only a few hundred years. A cycle called the "medieval warm period" began about 700 years ago and lasted about 200 years. The so-called little ice age followed and spanned the time from about 1400 A.D. to 1900. After a hundred years of relative warmth, we are now on the edge of a gradual cooling period. This cycle will take place with or without human influences. Unfortunately, the natural cooling phase will occur too slowly to counter the greenhouse—or warming—effect.

Climatologists find it difficult to demonstrate the links between carbon dioxide and rapid warming because little information is available. Indeed, the exact measurements of carbon dioxide in our atmosphere have been recorded for a short period of time—only the last 40 years. In addition, current technology cannot distinguish which climate trend could cause a very small temperature increase—such as one or two degrees Fahrenheit. Although climate models are intended to take into account most if not all small background fluctuations, they yield only rough approximations. This problem will continue until grid sizes are reduced and more powerful computers are developed.

There remain several reputable and qualified scientists who disagree with the idea that global warming is inevitable. They argue that the climate conditions are cyclic and that while global temperature has risen slightly over the past 100 years, it will decline again as it has done in the distant past. They point out that the predictions of a gradual but steady rise in temperature are derived from climate models that contain many questionable assumptions. For example, the rate of absorption of carbon dioxide by the oceans is a disputable factor. Those who believe that global warming is real argue that there is a wealth of evidence to support their position—such as the retreat of glaciers in the polar regions—that does not depend on the results of computer models.

Global Politics

As early as the 1970s, scientists and engineers recognized the difficulty of controlling carbon dioxide (CO_2) emissions. They also recognized the possibility that increases in CO_2 might lead to changes in the Earth's climate. To improve upon this worldwide problem, environmentalists sought to make the reduction of CO_2 emissions an international issue. In 1987, the directors of the Environment Programme of the United Nations called a conference to be held in Montreal, Canada. Technical experts from all corners of the world prepared what they called a Framework Convention on Climate Change. To attain a consensus among the national representatives, the delegates worded their suggestions in rather general terms. In 1992, the representatives endorsed the basic philosophy of the Montreal Convention at a meeting on sustainable economic growth in Rio de Janeiro.

The next step was to arrive at a more formal agreement. In 1997, delegates reached this goal during a meeting in Kyoto, Japan. The agreement, called the Kyoto Protocol, was signed by the U.S. delegate in 1998. At about the same time, more than 160 nations also became signatories. However, before the protocol would have the status of an international treaty, the national assembly of each nation must ratify the document.

In March 2001, the chief environmental officials of six highly industrialized countries met in Trieste, Italy, to reaffirm their countries' commitment to the protocol. The United States was one of the participants. A few days later, President George W. Bush announced that the protocol would not be submitted to the U.S. Senate for ratification. Many people around the world saw the lack of commitment by the United States as a serious weakening of the cooperative arrangements. Indeed, in 2004, representatives of the Russian Federation began to pull back from their earlier support of the protocol.

Economic considerations are the main reasons for withdrawal from the commitment. U.S. and Russian Federation officials claim that the protocol is unfair because CO_2 emission limits are imposed on highly industrialized nations while developing nations can delay such action. Other nations, too, see little urgency in correcting the CO_2 problem. They believe that costly delaying actions can be postponed because global warming is seen as a very gradual process. An additional reason to postpone actions concerns the fact that carbon dioxide is not a toxic gas and produces no dramatic symptoms such as an increase in dead trees or dead and dying fish washing up on shores. U.S. and Russian officials also give science-related justifications. Specifically, they maintain that new data from climate monitoring demonstrates that the early predictions of temperature increase have not been fulfilled.

When the interests of heavy industry and politics coincide, these powerful forces maintain that scientific research is faulty or incomplete. While this argument allows the government to postpone regulations, it also leads to calls for government support of improvements in the research efforts.

Research Initiatives

Detractors of the Kyoto Protocol argue that more research is needed before national policy decisions can be made. This position has led to the creation of two research and development organizations in the U.S. government, both coordinated

by the Office of Management and Budget in the Executive
Office of the President. One is the Climate Change Science Program and the other is the Climate Change Technology Program. Relevant executive agencies such as the National
Institute for Standards and Technology and the National Science Foundation are participants in both programs. The
National Aeronautics and Space Administration (NASA) has a
prominent role in the science program because of the orbital
satellites in its Earth Observation System. The core of the system is composed of three, city bus–sized satellites named Terra,
Aqua, and Aura that were launched successively in 2000, 2002
and 2004. Terra contains cameras, radars, and three other

*The inner workings of the Terra satellite being erected to a vertical orien-
tation so that the final assembly of the space vehicle can be completed.*
(Courtesy of the National Aeronautics and Space Administration)

monitoring devices that provide a continuous survey of conditions on the Earth's land surfaces. Aqua contains monitors that provide coverage of the oceans, including temperature of surface water, salinity, and color analyses to indicate the presence of pollution or the rapid growth of colonies of algae. Monitors in Aura cover the atmosphere and register the presence and amount of 19 gases, external temperatures, and the altitude of cloud tops found in the polar regions.

In addition, NASA officials are working toward the development of smaller, less expensive satellites. Two advanced versions—the *Lewis* and the *Clark* respectively—were launched in 2004. Each contains a package of miniaturized instruments to check atmospheric conditions. The instruments include X-ray detectors and monitors of the trace gases found in the atmosphere. Similarly, NASA is cooperating with the European Space Agency in the design and use of several sets of environmental satellites. The leading example is called Envisat and is similar in size and function to NASA's three large climate satellites.

Ground-Level Studies

The Department of Energy (DOE) is the lead agency for much of the ground-based research. Its priorities include the suppression of carbon dioxide emissions and the capture of carbon dioxide that enters the Earth's atmosphere. Research on the suppression of carbon dioxide is related to finding alternatives to coal as the fuel for electric power generation. Equally important is the development of techniques to remove some carbon dioxide from coal fire–generated gases. For example, some removal is possible if flue (chimney) gases are bubbled through special solutions before ascending the smokestack. These solutions contain calcium and a catalyst and together with the flue gases produce calcium carbonate, a product that can be recycled as an industrial raw material. Scientists are seeking additional catalysts to help change unusable or dangerous gases into usable or harmless products.

Once carbon dioxide enters the atmosphere, it is diluted by nitrogen and oxygen and therefore difficult to capture by artificial means. Green plants naturally perform that function by taking in some carbon dioxide to form sugars, starches, and cellulose. Oceans, however, cleanse the atmosphere of vast amounts of CO_2. Almost half of all the carbon dioxide that enters the atmosphere is eventually dissolved in ocean waters. Whether the oceans might become saturated at some time in the future is a prominent question for scientists.

The importance of the oceans' ability to capture and hold CO_2 has led some chemists to speculate about storing carbon dioxide at the bottoms of the deepest oceans. Once carbon dioxide is removed from flue gas, it can be compressed to form a liquid. This liquid is called supercritical because carbon dioxide—unlike many gases such as water vapor—does not naturally form a liquid. The artificially-formed, pressurized liquid can be injected into the depths of the ocean, where the combination of low temperature and high pressure tends to keep the blob of liquid carbon dioxide intact. According to current scientific research, such a blob will never dissolve.

On a still more speculative level, some atmospheric scientists have put forward the idea that global warming might be suppressed if global cooling could be increased. For example, some cooling takes place when massive clouds form after volcanic eruptions. Specialists wonder if the same effect could be accomplished by artificial means. They have noted that crystals are formed from some sulfur emissions. Such sulfur oxide crystals are highly reflective of sunlight and, when naturally transported to cloud tops, slow the effects of CO_2 and other greenhouse gases. If such a technique could be perfected, it would be a boon for the companies that burn coal to generate electricity. These industries produce relatively large amounts of both carbon dioxide and sulfur oxides. If one pollutant could counter the effects of another, no harm would be done to the environment. The acid rain produced by the sulfur oxides might also be overlooked since the cooling effect would be so beneficial. The whole concept fell apart, however, when atmospheric chemists pointed out that sulfur oxides are removed from the atmosphere by rainfall while most of the carbon dioxide remains in the air.

There are no cheap and easy ways to decrease the amount of carbon dioxide—or other greenhouse gases such as water vapor—in the atmosphere. Shifting from coal to natural gas for electricity generation would be helpful, but converting existing power plants to the new fuel would be costly and time consuming. Solving the dilemma of climate change will take time, new techniques, and the goodwill of all concerned.

12
Clean Energy

What can be done to prevent or minimize global warming? Industrialized nations—particularly the United States—must use less energy produced from fossil fuels. Five percent of the world's population lives in the United States. That 5 percent consumes 25 percent of the energy produced each year.

The simple act of switching off unnecessary electric lights will save a surprisingly large amount of energy. The use of fluorescent bulbs rather than incandescent bulbs will further increase conservation. Setting air-conditioning systems a few degrees higher in summer and heating systems a few degrees lower in winter will also save large amounts of electricity and fuel. All of these measures will reduce the need for energy. In turn, this reduction will lower the use of fossil fuels that produce atmospheric carbon dioxide.

Public Policy Issues

Both the depletion of the ozone layer and the increase in carbon dioxide are global issues. Indeed, present and future populations will suffer if there is no remedy. No one country can solve the problem. All people in all nations must work together.

Ideally, the United Nations should provide leadership for such a collaboration. However, the UN has a mixed record in dealing with difficult issues. For example, at the beginning of the ozone depletion crisis, the United Nations Environment Program (UNEP) was consistently slow in responding to scientific findings. UNEP conferences were held yearly, and delegates brought forth a wide range of views. Concluding statements usually called for more research, further information exchange, and additional meetings. Multinational treaties were rare.

In some ways, the situation in the United States parallels that in the United Nations. Citizens have conflicting ideas and interests concerning environmental issues. Moreover, agencies within the federal government advance a variety of ideas on public policy. Politicians and government administrators find it difficult to agree on solutions that require people to change their behavior. Today, federal agencies provide funds to study methods to generate energy by the use of low-polluting or nonpolluting materials.

Technical Responses

METHANE PRODUCTION

One of the most promising techniques is the use of carbon-based waste materials to produce methane (CH_4). Methane, a simple molecule made of one carbon and four hydrogen atoms, is an inflammable gas at room temperature. The gas can be used to fuel power plants and other systems that commonly use fossil fuels.

Natural gas, a cleaner and more efficient fossil fuel than coal or oil, is a source of methane. There are abundant supplies of natural gas in many parts of the world, including areas without coal or oil resources. Methane is easy and inexpensive to produce. Indeed, most carbon-based materials can be converted to methane by the natural action of bacteria.

Backyard gardeners can manufacture methane by mulching. Methane gas is a by-product of this process, in which grass cuttings, leaves, and other household garbage are dumped into

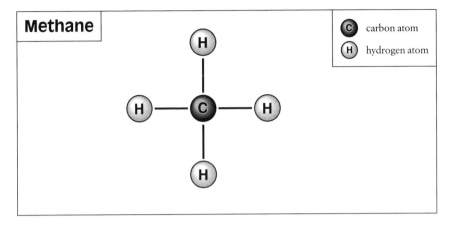

Natural gas is composed of methane, the simplest hydrocarbon molecule.

large metal containers or pits dug into the ground. Small amounts of fertilizer or other sources of nitrogen are added. Bacteria multiply rapidly in this medium and digest the mixture. After a period of time, the action of the bacteria reduces the material to a moist, porous, brown substance. When added to the garden, the mulch fertilizes and softens the soil.

Some caution is needed when methane is produced because this gas—like CO_2—is also a greenhouse gas. Backyard mulching systems usually allow methane to escape into the atmosphere. Some mulching systems now capture and compress the gas for use in backyard barbecues and winter fireplaces. However, large quantities of unrecoverable methane are produced by the digestive systems of cows and other animals. Unusable methane is also found during plant fermentation in wet rice paddies and other agricultural sources.

Methane is produced commercially by large farms and waste management companies. These organizations use sizable special chambers similar to those found in small backyard systems. Waste materials such as municipal garbage, straw, crushed cornstalks and cobs, and used paper are employed as mulch to produce methane. Indeed, this environmentally safe fuel can be quickly and easily produced as long as plants grow on the Earth.

Methane and other gaseous fuels have another major advantage. These gases can be used in an extremely efficient and cost-saving technology. Hot gases from the burning fuel cause a turbine to rotate. The turbine is connected to a generator that produces electric power. In turn, the exhaust gases from the same turbine are used to boil water that generates steam. The steam is used to turn another set of turbines and generate more electric power. Thus, gases from the burning fuel drive a turbine that generates energy, and exhaust gases from that turbine produce steam to create more energy. Manufacturers can use the same amount of fuel to produce almost twice the electricity and generate half the pollution.

REFORESTATION

In many parts of the world, programs of reforestation are becoming more prevalent. These programs address a variety of problems such as timber shortage, soil erosion, mud slides, and of increasing importance, the growing excess of CO_2. Trees, and to a lesser degree all plants, require CO_2 to grow and therefore absorb quantities of the gas.

In the United States, reforestation is practiced by timber and paper companies that harvest large numbers of trees. Federal law mandates that these companies replace trees cut on federal land administered by the Forest Service. For public relations, political, and economic reasons, many companies promote reforestation programs. Very large industrial firms often set up reforestation departments within their companies. Others engage small companies that provide the service of replanting forests. These companies specialize in developing tree stocks that are naturally resistant to disease and insect attacks. Their business is booming. One small Canadian company sold almost 400,000 tree seedlings in its sixth year of operation.

In recent years, individual states in the United States have become more active in caring for their timber resources. Several states, notably Washington and Oregon, have regulations restricting logging in sensitive areas. Many lumber companies use a method called clear-cutting. In clear-cutting, every tree in a designated area—regardless of size or condition—is cut down. The method is popular because the area can then be easily and completely cleared of the felled trees. Although the method saves money for timber companies, it is not good for the environment.

The soil in many northwestern states consists of a thin layer of topsoil that covers loose sand and gravel. Clear-cutting damages the root systems that helped retain the thin layer of top soil. Erosion, mud slides, and other ecological problems can result. In the state of Washington, the salmon industry is suffering from the results of clear-cutting. Loosened gravel and other matter enter the waterways and silts up, or clogs, streams where salmon spawn. As a result, the salmon population has been dramatically depleted.

Although reforestation offers a solution to some environmental problems, many ecologists have reservations about this approach. Scientists worry that it creates an artificial environment rather than a natural forest. Indeed, reforestation usually creates a monoculture—a forest planted with seedlings of the same age and type of tree. The new trees will succeed in absorbing CO_2. However, the reforested area may not provide the varied habitat needed by the creatures that populate a natural forest.

In the United States, the Sierra Club, the Audubon Society, and other well-known organizations promote tree-planting projects. Smaller groups such as the Global Relief Program are active in urban settings. However, many areas of the world are not interested in such projects. In some countries, more urgent problems give reforestation a low priority. In others, the original deforestation profoundly changed soil and water conditions, and growth of new forests is very difficult if not impossible. Some areas around the Mediterranean Sea fall into this category.

Unused land can revert to a forested area by a natural process. In New England states, a form of spontaneous reforestation can occur. Steep or rocky land reverts to scrub growth when taken out of cultivation. After many years, these plots may become fully diversified forest areas. Although some larger trees may be cut for firewood, the reforested area usually remains in an untamed condition.

In poorer countries of the world, the need for firewood is so great that land can rarely be reforested. Trees are cut down long before they reach maturity. However, in industrialized areas of Europe, uncultivated land is rarely stripped of saplings for firewood. Studies sponsored by the Finnish government suggest that the expansion of northern European forests is responsible for the absorption of 15 million tons of carbon dioxide every year. According to research sponsored by the U.S. Forest Service, spontaneous reforestation in the United States increases the absorption of excess CO_2.

The formation of peat allows forests in the world's temperate zones to retain a goodly amount of the excess CO_2. Peat is made of vegetable matter such as leaves and bark that have absorbed CO_2 during their lifetime. The vegetation falls to the forest floor and is gradually covered by earth. The mixture is slowly compressed by the weight of the soil. Early environmental studies of temperate-zone forests neglected to take into consideration the amount of carbon dioxide held by peat.

Northern, temperate forests—and the resultant peat—capture about one half as much carbon dioxide as do tropical rain forests. Because of year-round heat and rainfall, these trees grow at a far faster rate than those in colder areas. Consequently, replanting the rain forests is very important. Governments of tropical countries such as Brazil, India, and Thailand are making progress in controlling the development of industries using wood products. They, too, are requiring reforestation by logging companies.

Electric utility companies in Holland and other parts of the world are also sponsoring tropical reforestation. The government and power companies of New Zealand are planting 250,000 acres (100,000 hectares) of new trees every year. Major electric power companies in the United States have also begun to sponsor reforestation projects both locally and abroad. Managers of utility companies hope to balance the CO_2 generated by their power plants with the CO_2 absorbed by the trees that they plant. These reforestation projects are also a means to achieve public approval and gain permission to build new and larger power plants.

The amount of all forested land—especially rain forests—is declining every year. The forests are cut for timber, to supply firewood, to increase farmland, and to accommodate expanding urban areas. Although trees are being replanted in many areas, the speed of deforestation is far greater.

Alternative Power Sources

To reduce the generation of carbon dioxide, the use of fossil fuels must be curtailed. Nuclear power, water power, tidal power, and wind and solar energy can be employed to produce electricity that is vital to the economy without producing nitrogen oxides, sulfur dioxide, CO_2, or smoke particles. These alternative sources all have positive as well as negative consequences. However, they all serve as alternatives that curtail atmospheric pollution.

NUCLEAR POWER

For many, nuclear power is an attractive alternative to the burning of fossil fuels. Nuclear power plants produce no sulfur, no nitrogen oxides, and no carbon dioxide.

Nuclear power comes from heat energy generated when the atoms of the metals uranium or plutonium release parts of their substance. This breaking apart is called fission and happens spontaneously. The process is usually carefully controlled in a nuclear power plant. In spite of the accidents at Three Mile Island near Harrisburg, Pennsylvania, in March 1979, and at Chernobyl village in the Ukrainian Republic, on April 26, 1986, nuclear power is relatively safe. Many people forget that no deaths or cases of radiation disease resulted from the Three Mile Island event. The quantity of radiation released during that incident was smaller than the normal amount of natural radiation.

The Chernobyl accident, however, was a catastrophe. Many plant employees, rescue workers, cleanup specialists, and nearby residents died because of the disaster. Some died quickly, others after suffering from radiation sickness. Fallout covered thousands of square kilometers in several countries. Farms and villages in the immediate vicinity of the plant were evacuated and remain uninhabited to this day. All agree that the plant was poorly designed, poorly managed, and poorly operated.

The accident began on April 25, 1986. The reactor at Unit 4 was scheduled for a routine shutdown for cleaning and maintenance. Administrators on the day shift planned to conduct tests during the shutdown and turned off some of the safety devices. Then, the shutdown and the tests were delayed because Kiev, the largest city in Ukrainia (now Ukraine), needed more electrical power. A few hours later, the delay ended, and the tasks were resumed by a less-experienced night crew. When the plant was restarted, power generation began to decrease too rapidly. The workers tried to correct the problem and speeded the release of nuclear energy to produce more steam. The disconnected safety equipment did not warn the workers when the reactor began to overheat. Too late, water was fed into the system. The water turned into steam with explosive force. After more confusion, a second explosion lifted the protective cover from the reactor and allowed air to enter. An intense fire resulted, and clouds of radioactive materials were sent into the air. Chaos followed.

World opinion about the use of nuclear energy has been strongly affected by these two crises. The incident at Three Mile Island made it impossible to obtain public support for additional nuclear power plant construction in the United States. The accident at Chernobyl convinced many people in many countries that the advantages of nuclear power were seriously overshadowed by the risks.

However, several countries, including France and Japan, are heavily dependent on nuclear power for the bulk of their electricity and continue to build new plants. The leaders of these countries are neither ignorant nor reckless. They have carefully studied all facets of the problem. Indeed, the Japanese are highly sensitive to the dangers of atomic energy because of their experience with the atom bomb.

Today, high-tech nuclear power plants are designed to eliminate most of the errors attributed to machine malfunction or human mistakes. The new plants produce few pollutants. Although most environmental problems have been solved, one enormous difficulty remains. This challenge involves uranium rods—the fuel used to operate the power plant. When uranium rods are placed in the reactor core, they support a chain reaction that produces heat to make steam. The steam drives the turbines to generate electricity, which is distributed to commercial and domestic users in the area. The manufacturing process goes smoothly except for one detail. No one can decide where to dispose of the used atomic fuel rods.

When uranium rods have served their purpose and can no longer be used as fuel, they must be replaced. At present, the rods are removed from the reactor core and stored underwater in trenches at the site of the power plant. However, the used rods remain radioactive. For 40 years, officials of the U.S. Department of Energy have spent vast amounts of money searching for a safe, acceptable location to bury those spent—

but highly dangerous—fuel rods. The most suitable location seems to be in the mountains of central Nevada. Naturally, the people of Nevada are not pleased to be the hosts for nuclear materials. Long legal battles are likely now that the federal government has chosen central Nevada as the final resting place for radioactive waste. Meanwhile, the amount of spent fuel continues to increase.

In contrast to nuclear fission, producing electricity by the process of nuclear fusion has greater appeal. Fusion is the same nuclear process that takes place in the Sun and that produces the heat that sustains life on Earth. The merging (or fusion) of two hydrogen atoms to form one helium atom generates a great amount of heat energy. The heat can be used to produce steam. Hydrogen—the only ingredient needed to begin the process—is in limitless supply. Helium—the result of the process—is harmless and nonpolluting. However, a system to fuse the hydrogen atoms requires costly apparatus and huge amounts of electricity. So far, the electricity required to run the system exceeds the quantity produced. Consequently, there is a net loss. Much more research is needed to achieve a practical system for generating electricity from nuclear fusion.

WATER POWER

For untold ages, the power of water was used to perform simple tasks. A wheel placed in a swiftly moving stream or river was turned by the force of the rushing water. Waterwheels often provided the energy to grind grain into flour. Today, most water power is generated by large dams built to control the flow of a river. A dam is constructed across a narrow river valley, blocking the river's course. A lake is formed behind the dam. The surface of the lake is higher than that of the natural riverbed. When the water is released, the torrent flows downstream through large pipes connected to giant turbines within the dam. The rushing water spins the turbines that rotate the electric generators. The water-generated electricity—called hydroelectric power—is produced without the use of fossil fuels.

Unfortunately, this environmentally safe procedure has some negative side effects. When the flow of a river is halted by a dam, silt, sand, and clay normally carried by the water settle out and accumulate in the lake. After a while, the silt must be dredged (removed) from the lake. Dams also interfere with the movement of fish, especially salmon. In the Northwest, salmon breeding is impaired, and the salmon population has declined in recent years. Scientists and environmentalists are seeking solutions to this problem.

Hydroelectric power accounts for about 8 percent of the electricity generated in the United States. Although additional

Using energy sources that are pollution-free does not always require a highly technical approach—as demonstrated by this simple water wheel.
(Courtesy of Gus Strangeland)

Hydroelectric Power

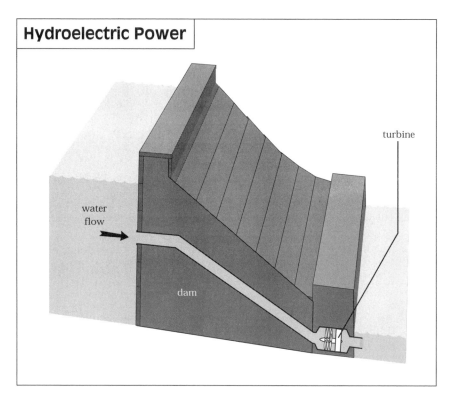

This sketch shows an internal cross section of the dam and how the flow of water is directed to a turbine that drives an electric generator.

expansion is possible, most of the better dam sites are already in use. Flat or gently rolling land is not suitable as the site of a dam. In order to generate the rush of water necessary to rotate the turbines, the level of the lake must be much higher than the level of the riverbed. Also, level land along a river is frequently very fertile. The flooding caused by dam construction can take important agricultural acreage out of production.

The Electric Consumers Protection Act (1986), states that water-powered electric plants must undergo an environmental impact analysis before gaining a license renewal. Preservation of wildlife habitats and consideration of agricultural irrigation have limited the upgrading of some existing plants. In the United States, electricity produced by hydroelectric plants has actually declined since 1986.

On a worldwide basis, water power has expanded rapidly since the 1950s. However, other means of generating electricity have expanded even more rapidly. Therefore, the proportion of electricity produced by water power has declined to about 20 percent of worldwide production.

Opportunities for large-scale expansion of hydroelectric power facilities are present in many developing countries. However, the issue of environmental protection has caused leaders of these countries to be cautious about new projects. Today, officials from industrialized countries are considering new programs to help develop and finance water-power facilities in those areas.

To support such developments, scientists and engineers have begun research programs such as surveying prospective dam sites. Fortunately, recent technology has facilitated the construction of economical, small-scale, hydroelectric stations in remote areas. A World Bank survey covering 31 developing countries reveals that power generation in these settings has doubled over the past 10 years.

TIDAL AND OCEAN WAVE POWER

The power of ocean tides is considerable. The rush of incoming and outgoing tides generates the same amount of power as the work of countless dams. If this enormous force could be harnessed in an economical manner, tidal power would be another clean source of energy. For the past 20 years or so, tidal power has received enthusiastic publicity. At present, however, there are only two major tidal power facilities in the world. One is located on the northwestern coast of France and the other in Canada on the Atlantic coast of Nova Scotia.

A special kind of dam called a "barrage" is used to capture the power of the tides. As high tide comes in, gates in the barrage are opened. The rush of water rotates the turbines at the sides of the gates. When the tide is fully in, the gates are closed, and the water is trapped until low tide. At low tide, the water within the barrage is higher than the water beyond. The gates are reopened, and water rushes back toward the ocean. The torrent of water again turns the wheels of the turbines. Therefore, the turbines generate electricity during the surge of both high and low tides.

The production of electricity by tidal power is limited to eight or 10 hours each day. The facilities are expensive to construct and operate. In order to justify such an investment, the tides at the site must rise at least 15 feet (5 m) or so. Since most tides range between three and four feet (about 1 m), most seashore areas are unsuitable for such projects. Technical experts predict that no more than 1 percent of the world's power needs can be provided by the tides.

Many different devices have been invented to take advantage of the untapped energy generated by ocean waves. So far, these methods have produced electricity on a relatively small scale. However, the concept appeals to inventors who see wave power as free and nonpolluting. Consequently, research programs of varying size and scope are under way in Japan, Norway, Denmark, and India as well as in the United Kingdom and the United States.

The difference between the temperatures of surface water and deep water has been considered a possible source of energy. Although the idea was conceived in the 1880s, no project was undertaken until 1930. Unfortunately, that system consumed more electric power than it generated. A second project was planned for a ship anchored off the coast of Brazil. The work was abandoned when the ship was wrecked by a storm. At present, the U.S. Department of Energy and other organizations are doing research on the subject.

Although ocean power is freely available, the techniques to capture this power are very complex. Indeed, the power of the oceans will not be harnessed until conventional sources become far more expensive.

GEOTHERMAL POWER

A layer of intensely hot, partially melted rock called magma lies below the crust of the Earth. In some locations, narrow faults in the crust allow water to seep down near the magma, heat to the boiling point, and rise to the surface of the Earth as steam. This is the origin of the hot springs and geysers found in Yellowstone Park. In places such as Iceland the faults are common, and many hot springs have been formed. Their steam is harnessed to drive electric generators. Some homes in Iceland are heated directly by water piped from the hot springs.

Large geothermal electric plants are expensive to build and operate. In addition, few areas are suitable. Geothermal energy will never account for more than a modest proportion of all energy production.

WIND POWER

Windmills generate energy to perform several kinds of work. Modern windmills are fairly high structures with blades attached to a shaft near the top. The blades are driven by the wind and power various kinds of machinery.

Archaeologists believe that the Babylonians built windmills as early as 1700 B.C. However, the first documented windmills were constructed in Persia (Iran) in 644 A.D. They were strange structures with the blades set parallel to the ground and attached to a short shaft. The shaft was connected directly to a small millstone used to grind grain into flour. Standard or vertical windmills were designed to copy the action of water mills. The wind-driven blades are attached to a horizontal shaft that is connected by gears to another shaft. This shaft activates a variety of devices. About 900 years ago, windmills became a popular source of power in Europe. The famous windmills of Holland are used to mill grain and to pump water from low-lying areas. Windmills have been used to drive machines such as the looms that weave fabric. Since 1890, they have been used to generate electricity. This application was first tried on the flat plains of Denmark.

In the United States, lumber companies used windmills to run sawmills. Farmers in the Midwest have used windmills to generate electricity and pump water from deep wells since the 1920s. Most windmills were relatively ugly structures of galvanized iron. Each stood about 25 feet (7.5 m) high and was topped with a multibladed fan. They creaked and groaned in the high prairie winds as they pumped well water for domestic use and into troughs for farm animals.

The petroleum shortage of the 1970s made everyone conscious of the dependence on Middle Eastern oil. This problem caused some inventors to think about harnessing wind energy. The systems developed during the oil crisis are far more elegant than the old farm windmills.

Top officials of the U.S. Department of Energy are encouraging the use of windmills to generate electric power in two different settings. On privately owned rural or semirural property, officials hope that owners of land not connected to power lines will attempt to generate their own electricity. Then, utility companies will not be required to extend expensive transmission equipment.

Even if the rural site is connected to power lines, a windmill system can conserve or replace fossil fuels. The property owner can generate part of the needed electricity by using a windmill and buy the rest from a utility company. In some places, surplus wind-generated electricity can be sold to a power company.

Indeed, many different arrangements are possible. The windmill owner can achieve complete energy independence by storing surplus energy in batteries. Heavy-duty battery packs, similar to those used to power golf carts, hold enough electric-

A modern geothermal facility in New Zealand (Courtesy of the National Archives and Records Administration)

ity to last three or four days. Diesel engines or ordinary gasoline engines can be used as emergency electric generators.

Conditions must be just right for the household windmill to be a wise investment. If electricity rates are high, purchasing and maintaining the equipment may be economically sound. However, the site must be very windy, and the system must be tall enough (about 30 feet, or 9 m) to catch the wind. In addition, the location must be far enough from neighbors so that the noise will not be a nuisance. If these conditions are met, each privately owned windmill will lower the output of carbon dioxide by two tons per year. That is the amount of CO_2 generated by a conventional power company to produce a family's yearly electrical supply.

The most important use for windmills is a wind-driven power plant that takes the place of a conventionally fueled utility company. A large number of windmills are erected on pylons that stand 40 feet (12 m) or higher and are spaced about 100 feet (30 m) apart. Each windmill can generate as much as 500 kilowatts of power. When many windmills are linked together into a power grid, they can supply electricity to a modest-sized community and eliminate the need for a fossil-fueled power plant.

A site for a windmill farm should be at least 50 acres (20 ha) in size. However, the land under the pylons need not be idle. It can be cultivated for crops or used as pasture land. Although the windmills produce some noise, the sound is not much greater than that of a busy office. One drawback is the danger to birds. They do not always see the whirling blades and fly into them. Scientists from the U.S. Department of Energy and the National Audubon Society are working on this problem.

The windmill in the background at this farm home is used to drive a water pump that brings well water to the surface. (Courtesy of the Agricultural Research Service)

A large wind farm in California. Such an array of windmills can generate enough electricity for a whole community. (Courtesy of the U.S. Department of Energy)

SOLAR POWER

Scientists have devised two types of solar energy systems. The older system uses the Sun to directly generate heat. Such systems can be quite modest. A series of curved reflectors focus the Sun's rays on a central pipe that holds water or some other fluid. Heated water can be used directly for household purposes such as bathing and washing dishes.

Slightly more elaborate solar energy systems are used to store heat. The heated fluid is passed through many channels in a large ceramic block. Such blocks will hold heat for several hours, so there can be hot water after the Sun sets. By eliminating the need for a hot water system that uses electricity or natural gas, a small reduction in carbon dioxide generation is achieved. Some larger installations have been adopted by home owners to provide home heating in the winter. However, the need for home heat is greatest when the sunshine is weakest and the cloud cover is most extensive.

Alternatives to providing heat to individual homes have been adopted by some electric utility companies on an experimental basis. These companies use large numbers of mirrors focused on a target container. The target material, which is often metallic sodium, is made very hot by these concentrated rays. When that material is passed through a device like a radiator, it can heat water to make steam. Then, the steam is used to drive a turbine that turns an electric generator.

Each mirror in the array of cup-shaped mirrors automatically tracks the Sun and focuses the Sun's energy to heat water to makes steam. The steam is used to generate electricity. (Courtesy of the Sandia Laboratory, U.S. Department of Energy)

The Helios *flying wing was designed to determine the practicality of using solar-electric energy to power a pilotless aircraft. The vehicle reached record altitudes in several test flights but later crashed into the Pacific Ocean in June 2004.* (Courtesy of the National Aeronautics and Space Administration)

The other type of panel is used to generate electricity directly from the Sun's rays. This process, called the photoelectric effect, uses panels that are about three feet (1 m) wide and six feet (2 m) high. Each panel faces the Sun and is divided into hundreds of small cells. Each cell contains a thin layer of silicon on top of a thin layer of metal. These layers are backed by a ceramic wafer called a semiconductor. When sunlight strikes the silicon, it jars some electrons from the silicon atoms. The electrons move through the metal layer into and through the semiconductor, and they then flow into an electric wire behind the semiconductor. This electron flow produces an electric current.

This is the technology used by satellites, space stations, and the robot landers that go to other planets. It is very clean and safe and can continue to work without moving parts or any adjustments for years. However, each panel generates only a small amount of electricity.

At present, commercial solar-generated power has been limited to medium-sized plants located in sites in the deserts of the southwestern United States and a few sunny countries. The electricity produced is relatively expensive because of the high cost of the panels. However, work goes forward on developing better methods to tap the Sun's energy.

Hydrogen as Fuel

Some clean sources of energy such as tidal power, wind power, and sun power produce electricity on a variable schedule. The tides run twice a day. The winds are undependable. The Sun cannot generate energy on cloudy days or at night. Hydrogen, another clean energy source, is always available. Hydrogen can be burned to serve any purpose requiring heat—including the production of electric power.

Hydrogen (H) can be made from ordinary water (H_2O) by the use of electricity. When an electric current is passed through the water, the hydrogen (H) portion of the molecule is separated from the oxygen (O). Since both oxygen and hydrogen are gases at room temperatures, they bubble up and break through the surface of the water. The gas can be captured in containers and stored for later use.

General acceptance of hydrogen-generated power will take many years. Industrialized countries have a huge investment in the production of energy by fossil fuels. Companies that mine and transport coal, explore for oil and natural gas, dig wells, and build pipelines would be financially weakened by a switch to hydrogen. Many other industries would be adversely affected. All the furnaces and boilers used to make steam for turbine generators would become obsolete. Automobile, truck, and tractor engines would be worth less than they are worth now. Indeed, huge investments would be lost if fossil fuels were replaced by hydrogen.

At present, hydrogen is about four to five times as expensive as methane or natural gas. However, it generates about three times as much energy per pound. Engineers and economists expect that hydrogen-produced energy will be priced competitively in about 50 years.

The use of such an alternative power source will be especially advantageous to many developing countries. Many of these areas are near the equator, where solar energy can be harnessed more consistently than in temperate countries. In addition, those nations have less capital invested in industries devoted to the use of fossil fuels. Consequently, fewer economic barriers would hinder the conversion to hydrogen-generated power. If the leaders of developing countries focus on developing hydrogen technologies, their countries could lead the movement to achieve bountiful, pollution-free energy.

There are many ways to reduce or control atmospheric pollution. Some require a reduction in industrial productivity and, perhaps, a decrease in general prosperity. Others might involve major changes in lifestyle.

The ways that would cause the least disturbance to the economy or to individual lifestyles are the alternative energy sources that could substitute for fossil fuels. At present, most alternative energy sources cost more than fossil fuels. However, surveys reveal that people will accept higher prices for utilities and manufactured products if the net outcome is a cleaner, less polluted atmosphere.

Fuel Cells

Some political leaders have proposed that the best way to achieve a hydrogen economy is through the development and adoption of fuel cells as a source of electricity. Fuel cells generate direct current by oxidizing hydrogen. The current from a fuel cell can be used to charge a battery, and that means that energy can be stored until it is needed—to run an electric motor, for example.

Hydrogen can be produced by activating a positive and a separate negative electrode immersed in water. The water (H_2O) is split into H_2 and O, both of which are gases. The fuel cell simply reverses this process—with complications. Specifically, the hydrogen must be kept from direct contact with the oxygen. An explosion can result if the two chemicals are mixed together. So, the hydrogen is injected into little channels that have been etched on the face of the positive electrode made of a metal such as copper. The oxygen source (normal air) is channeled on the face of a negative electrode, and the two electrodes are separated by a membrane (similar to plastic wrap) that is coated with a powdered platinum compound that helps control the reaction. The bare apparatus looks like a metal sandwich. The result of the merger of the hydrogen with the oxygen within the sandwich is the generation of a voltage between the two electrodes and the production of hot water—but no pollutants.

The politicians and others who favor the development of fuel cells do not often remind the citizens that more electricity (or some other source of energy such as fossil fuels) had to be used to make the hydrogen. More energy is also needed to dis-

A miniature hydrogen fuel cell was used to power the prize-winning model car built by students at the Doolen Middle School in Tucson, Arizona. The student standing second from the left in the photo holds the model car. (Courtesy of the Renewable Energy Laboratories, U.S. Department of Energy)

tribute the hydrogen to users, and no mention is made of the cost of manufacturing the complete fuel cell that is composed of dozens of the metal sandwiches. Indeed, the whole procedure yields a net loss of energy. However, there is some hope that the tangle can be straightened-out.

Biochemists at the University of Wisconsin have proposed a possible solution. They are testing a new type of fuel cell that uses carbon monoxide (CO) as one ingredient. Carbon monoxide is a troublesome waste product from the burning of fossil fuels. The other ingredient is a crystalline material formed by a metal atom, such as silver or iron, plus some water molecules.

Such crystals are called polyoxometalates. When introduced into the metal sandwich arrangement of a fuel cell, the carbon monoxide is induced to take up an oxygen atom to form carbon dioxide, and the result is a voltage. Since carbon monoxide is a toxic waste material, changing it into carbon dioxide is a good thing—even though carbon dioxide is a greenhouse gas. Using such advanced technologies, there is still hope that the fuel cell can provide a step toward a pollution-free energy system.

Hybrid Cars

Hybrid cars are no dream of the future. They are on the roads now. More than 100,000 such vehicles were sold in the United States between 2000 and 2004.

These vehicles combine two well-established methods of propulsion: the internal combustion engine and the electric motor. The combination works far better than does each separately.

Hybrid vehicles come in two versions, parallel and series. In the parallel version, both the internal combustion engine and the electric motor can power the wheels. Usually, the internal combustion engine provides all the propulsion. The electric motor is activated when additional power is needed for hill climbing or quick acceleration. Also, the internal combustion engine is connected to a generator that recharges the battery that provides the electricity to run the electric motor.

In the series version, the electric motor provides all the propulsion. The internal combustion engine only drives a generator to keep the battery charged. One advantage is that no gear shifting is needed. The power output of the electric motor can be controlled by electronic means, leading to a lower cost of manufacture because a complicated transmission system is not needed.

Both types of hybrid vehicles are more efficient because the internal combustion engine can be kept relatively small. Also, the internal combustion engine in a hybrid can run on conventional gasoline or compressed natural gas (methane). Alternatively, the engine can be a diesel and run on a mix of petroleum and vegetable oils. All the options yield benefits of lower emissions. The next step is to develop similar propulsion systems for larger, heavier vehicles such as buses and tractor-trailer trucks.

Glossary

abatement   The reduction or elimination of pollution.

acid rain   Rainfall having more than normal acidity, most often generated by oxides of sulfur and nitrogen in the atmosphere.

acute exposure   Contact with a harmful pollutant for a period of less than 24 hours.

adsorb   The process whereby a solid object like a grain of sand holds a thin layer of another substance on its surface.

adsorber   An emission control device that removes harmful chemicals from a flow of gases by attachment to a solid material such as activated charcoal.

aerosol   A very fine mist of droplets that stays airborne for an extended time.

air mass   A large body of air that has relatively uniform features. Within the mass, temperature and barometric pressure are similar.

albedo   The amount of reflected energy compared to the total energy received by a surface; usually expressed as a percentage.

allowance   An amount of pollutant permitted from a source such as a power plant based on the plant's history of emissions. The allowance is expressed in units such as one ton of sulfur dioxide per year. If a plant does not need all its units, they can be traded or sold to other polluters.

anticyclone   A large air mass characterized by high barometric pressure with winds moving in a clockwise direction in the Northern Hemisphere and counterclockwise in the Southern Hemisphere.

barometric pressure The weight of a column of air above a specified area; measured in centimeters of the height of a column of mercury forced upward in a glass tube from which the air has been removed.

carbon dioxide (CO_2) A colorless and odorless gas produced by a fire.

coalescence The merger of two small water droplets to form a larger droplet.

cold front The boundary between a mass of cold air and a mass of warm air whereby the cold air usually underruns the warm air, pushing it up.

composite weather map A representation in a single image of several conditions simultaneously—such as air pressure, moisture level, and temperature.

condensation The process by which a vapor becomes a liquid or a solid.

convection Movement of material away from a heat source toward a cooler region. Heat energy is transferred by such movement.

convergence The narrowing of a flow, as when water runs down a drain.

cyclone An area of low barometric pressure in which the winds blow in a counterclockwise direction in the Northern Hemisphere and clockwise in the Northern Hemisphere.

deposition The process whereby chemicals move from the atmosphere to the Earth's surface.

depression Another name for a cyclone.

dew point The temperature at which water commences to condense from the air onto a solid surface; the point at which the relative humidity reaches 100 percent.

diesel engine An engine in which the fuel is ignited by the heat generated by compression rather than by an electric spark as in an internal combustion engine.

eddy Small shift in the movement of air currents.

ethanol   An alcohol with two carbon atoms per molecule that results from the fermentation of plant materials.

evaporation   The process by which a liquid is changed into a gas.

exhaust gas recirculation   A technique whereby exhaust gases are mixed in with the intake of fuel and air so that contaminants such as nitrogen oxides are more thoroughly consumed before emission into the atmosphere.

fly ash   Airborne particles from burning coal or other solid fuels.

fossil fuels   Fuels that are the remains of once living matter: coal, oil, and natural gas.

front   The border or boundary between two air masses.

greenhouse effect   The action of gases in the atmosphere that retain and re-emit radiant heat that would otherwise escape into space.

greenhouse gases   Carbon dioxide, methane, chlorofluorocarbons, nitrogen oxides, and water vapor.

humidity   A measure of the amount of water vapor in the atmosphere.

infrared   Light that carries heat energy and is not visible to humans.

inversion   A layer of warmer air on top of a layer of cooler air.

isobar   A line connecting two points on a weather map that have the same barometric pressure.

jet stream   A strong flow of air in the stratosphere that moves from west to east in the Northern Hemisphere and that often marks the boundary between polar air and tropical air.

latitude   The distance north or south from the equator measured in degrees of the circumference of a circle.

meteorology   The study of the Earth's atmosphere, with particular emphasis on weather forecasting.

monsoon   A seasonal wind usually accompanied by heavy rains.

nitrogen oxides   A group of gases that can make rain acid and which contribute to the formation of smog.

organic compounds   Chemicals formed mainly of carbon, hydrogen, oxygen, and nitrogen that originate in living creatures.

photochemical reactions   Chemical processes that are driven by light energy, as in the impact of sunlight on mixtures of nitrogen oxides and incompletely oxidized organic fuels such as gasoline vapors to form smog.

precipitation   Rain, sleet, or snow.

radon   A nonreactive, inert but radioactive gas that results from the decay of the radium in rocks and soils.

relative humidity   The amount of water in the atmosphere relative to the maximum amount that could be held at the prevailing temperature—expressed as a percentage.

sanctions   Actions taken, such as the imposition of a fine, in response to violation of a regulation.

semiconductor   A device that allows an electric current to flow in one direction only.

smog   Originally, a mixture of smoke and fog; now also refers to a mixture of ozone, oxides of nitrogen, and particles made up of carbon compounds.

squall line   The boundary between converging air currents where heavy, sudden rain storms erupt.

stratosphere   The layer of atmosphere above the troposphere where the air is very thin and calm conditions are normal.

synoptic   The summarization of much weather information, often in graphic format as a weather map.

thermal   A relatively restricted and well-bounded column of rising an over a warm area.

topography   The configuration of a surface, such as the surface of the Earth with its natural ups and downs as well as its man-made features.

troposphere   The lowest layer of the atmosphere, from the surface to a height of from six to 12 miles (10–20 km).

warm front   The boundary between an advancing mass of warm air sloping upward from the ground and pushing into a mass of cold air.

wind   The movement of air relative to the surface of the Earth, described in terms of the location of origin so that a northeasterly wind comes out of the northeast.

wind shear   Sharp change in the direction or the speed of the wind.

Further Reading

Allaby, Michael. *Encyclopedia of Weather and Climate.* 2 vols. New York: Facts On File, 2002. Almost 3,000 entries that cover a full range of topics in atmospheric science, as well as storms having names and capsule biographies of key contributors to the science.
———. *Fog, Smog, and Poisoned Rain.* New York: Facts On File, 2003. A very thorough coverage for young adults of atmospheric phenomena of all kinds. Both natural and man-made events are discussed, with particular emphasis on technical remedies to pollution problems.

Baines, John. *Conserving the Atmosphere.* Austin, Tex.: Steck-Vaughn, 1990. This book focuses on the causes of various forms of air pollution. Carefully written and well illustrated, it contains a useful listing of foundations and other organizations dedicated to the preservation of the environment.

Blashfield, Jean F., and Wallace B. Black. *Global Warming.* Chicago: Children's Press, 1991. This title includes sections on hands-on experiences and experiments that can be conducted in a classroom setting.

Burroughs, William J. *The Climate Revealed.* Cambridge: Cambridge University Press, 1999. This is a well-illustrated and comprehensive book on climate science that also covers weather issues.

Chapman, Mathew, and Rob Bowden. *Air Pollution: Our Impact on the Planet.* Austin, Tex.: Raintree Steck-Vaughn Publishers, 2002. A straightforward and balanced review of the main issues. Extensive use of condensed sidebars, plus varied and colorful illustrations make for heightened reader interest.

Haley, James, ed. *Global Warming: Opposing Viewpoints.* New York: Greenhaven Press, 2001. The book presents cogent articles from several different authors representing a variety of points of view—thus providing a well-balanced picture of the causes of global warming and the steps to be taken to bring the process under control.

———. *Pollution: Current Controversies*. New York: Greenhaven Press, 2002. Captures the essence of the present political debates about pollution—the causes and the cures. Includes articles by activists, industrialists, and academic scientists, as well as representatives of government agencies.

Kahl, Jonathan D. *Hazy Skies: Weather and the Environment*. Minneapolis, Minn.: Lerner Publishers, 1998. Clear coverage of the significant events in the history of air pollution and the attempts to come to a scientific understanding of the causes and the remedies that technology might provide.

Lambert, David, and Ralph Hardy. *Weather and Its Works*. New York: Facts On File, 1984. Written and first published in Great Britain, this volume has a truly global orientation. The authors do a particularly good job of distinguishing among the various climate types around the world. This book is now out of print; however, it may still be in libraries.

Mason, John. *Weather and Climate*. Englewood Cliffs, N.J.: Silver Burdett Press, 1991. This book is written simply, with plentiful illustrations. Its broad coverage includes most aspects of atmospheric pollution and the technical means for observing changes in the atmosphere.

Miller, Christina G., and Louise A. Berry. *An Alert: Rescuing the Earth's Atmosphere*. New York: Simon & Schuster, 1996. A young adult book on air pollution and political solutions.

Schaefer, Vincent J., and John A. Day. *A Field Guide to the Atmosphere*. Boston: Houghton Mifflin, 1983. One of the well-known series of Peterson Field Guides, this copiously illustrated handbook concentrates on helping the reader distinguish between different types of clouds and between different types of snow and other forms of precipitation. The first author was a pioneer in weather modification.

Warwick, Hugh, and Alison Doig. *Smoke: The Killer in the Kitchen: Indoor Air Pollution in Developing Countries*. London: ITDG, 2004. Conditions in developing countries can force the extensive use of open fires, with a variety of fuels for cooking and heating. For years, the use of such fires was taken for granted. Now, the threat to health presented by particulate matter in smoke causes concern on the part of public health experts around the world.

Weather and Climate. Alexandria, Va.: Time Life Books, 1991. This heavily illustrated book mainly presents explanations of the how and why of weather and climate effects.

Web Sites

The following list contains a sample of sites on the World Wide Web that provide up-to-date information on atmospheric pollution, climate change, and weather phenomena. The addresses are valid as of April 2005. However, owing to the nature of the Internet and the rapid changes that occur there, URLs may have changed since this book was published. If so, the site's name or topic can be used as a search term that should lead to alternative sites and links to other relevant information. Also, many of the government agencies mentioned in the book are not covered in the list since they are easily found by using their initials as the search term. For example, the home page of the Environmental Protection Agency will be retrieved by searching the acronym EPA.

Activist Organizations

Climateark: Climate Change Portal. An advocacy group pushing energy conservation. The group also provides current news bulletins on climate issues. URL: http://www.climateark.org. Accessed April 19, 2005.

The Climate Trust. This organization originated in Oregon and has spread throughout the United States. Its goal is to obtain agreements from private firms (mainly utility companies) so that their use of environmental credits will achieve a reduction of carbon dioxide emissions. URL: http://www.climatetrust.org. Accessed April 19, 2005.

CURES: Citizens United for Renewable Energy and Sustainability. A European organization of ordinary citizens who promote energy conservation practices. URL: http://www.cures-network.org. Accessed April 19, 2005.

Environmental Investigation Agency. A privately supported group that tries to uncover the activities of those who poach endangered species, such as the tiger of India and the rhinoceros of Africa. The group also has been active in tracking black marketers and the smugglers of chlorofluorocarbons. URL: http://www.ecocrimes. org. Accessed April 19, 2005.

Green Mountain Club. Members of this club are mountain trail hikers. Many are concerned about air quality in the highlands, where pollution tends to be concentrated. Club officials lobby for stronger air pollution controls by federal and state agencies and testify at congressional hearings. URL: http://www.greenmountainclub.org. Accessed April 19, 2005.

League of Conservation Voters. Collects and publishes the environmental voting records of members of the U.S. Congress and U.S. Senate and also publicizes significant congressional actions that affect the environment. URL: http://www.lcv.org. Accessed April 19, 2005.

National Audubon Society. Has more than 500,000 members who are interested in the protection of the environment and the creatures that live therein. URL: http://www.audubon.org. Accessed April 19, 2005.

Natural Resources Defense Council. Collects and publishes news and background information on public policy issues that relate to the environment. URL: http://www.nrdc.org. Accessed April 19, 2005.

Government and International Organizations

The BOREAS (Boreal Ecosystem–Atmosphere Study) Project. A Canadian-American collaboration for the study of the exchange of trace gases such as carbon dioxide between the atmosphere and boreal forests. URL: http://www-eosdis.ornl.gov/BOREAS/bhs/ BOREAS_Home.html. Accessed April 19, 2005.

Illinois Environmental Protection Agency. This site is representative of the way states work to prevent or correct air pollution. URL: http://www.epa.state.il.us/air/ozone/exceedances.html. Accessed April 19, 2005.

Institute for Global Environmental Strategies. An organization that helps coordinate environmental research and the pursuit of practical means to protect the environment. URL: http://www.strategies.org. Accessed April 19, 2005.

International Energy Agency's Solar Heating and Cooling Programme. Part of the Organization for Economic Cooperation and Development. Staff members collect and distribute information on climate change. URL: http://www.iea-shc.org. Accessed April 19, 2005.

International Geosphere-Biosphere Programme. Collects and processes scientific information about the chemical and biological interactions that relate to global climate change. URL: http://www.igbp.kva.se. Accessed April 19, 2005.

Ozone Secretariat. A branch of the Environment Program of the United Nations. The Ozone Secretariat was established to help promote the goals and enforce the restrictions set down by the Montreal Convention on ozone depletion. URL: http://www.unep.org/ozone. Accessed April 19, 2005.

U.S. Government Accountability Office. Staff members conduct evaluation studies of the actions and programs of federal agencies on a wide range of issues, including the environment. URL: http://www.gao.gov. Accessed April 19, 2005.

Academic Research Organizations

Air Pollution Research Center. Located at the University of California at Riverside, the APRC performed the first studies of the effects of smog on growing plants. This work led to the establishment of the center in 1961 and its continuation as a university regents program to the present. URL: http://www.aprc.ucr.edu. Accessed April 19, 2005.

Columbia University Center for Carbon Management. Part of the Earth Engineering Center and the Department of Earth &

Environment Engineering. A group of researchers seeking ways to reduce the emissions of carbon dioxide from coal. URL: http://www.ccm.columbia.edu. Accessed April 19, 2005.

Meteorology Department at the University of Maryland, College Park. Conducted the post-blackout study of power plant emissions in 2003 and 2004. URL: http://www.atmos.umd.edu. Accessed April 19, 2005.

National Center for Atmospheric Research and the UCAR Office of Programs. Based at the University of Colorado at Boulder, this is a group of cooperating universities that educates students in the atmospheric sciences and provides support for the research projects of both faculty and students. URL: http://www.ucar.edu. Accessed April 19, 2005.

Index

Italic page numbers indicate illustrations.